The Guardian

→ more COR REC- TIONS & → Clarific -ations two

Corrections & Clarifications

Ian Mayes

★✦✱✖✩✩✱★✳

Published by Guardian Newspapers Limited,
119 Farringdon Road, London EC1R 3ER.
Distributed by Atlantic Books, a division of Grove Atlantic, Ltd

ISBN: 1 84354 173 4

Printed and bound by Biddles

For Hannah, William, Isabella and Harry

Contents

Foreword

Alan Rusbridger

There was once a time when the newspaper business looked a bit like an inverted funnel. At the pinnacle were the sources of information – Westminster, Whitehall, the professions, the courts, the church and so on. At the base of the neck sat the journalist, sifting, sorting, controlling. And at the bottom was the reader. Thousands – millions – of them.

It was a model which survived very nicely for the best part of four centuries. It was not an entirely one-way process. Readers were acknowledged as a source of news, and were even encouraged to write letters on matters of opinion. But that – for most newspapers, most of the time – was about as far as it went.

If you sought a graphic representation of a newspaper today I think it more likely that it would look like a cross section of a grapefruit. The newspaper would be at the core, surrounded by an outer circle of readers, with various segments in the middle. The key is the reader. There is a vast difference between a reader armed with pen and paper (old funnel model) and a reader armed with a computer (grapefruit model). The pen-and-paper reader is unlikely to be in touch with any other readers. He has no way of telling if other readers are as pleased or outraged by a particular article. He is unlikely to have much access to direct sources of information of his own. Short of going to the PCC or to law he has no redress against a newspaper if the editor chooses not to publish a letter.

Compare the computer-reader. There is endless scope for her to talk and compare notes with other readers. She can immediately check her newspaper's coverage not only against other media organisations around the world, but also against original sources – often the same sources used by the journalist. She can post views or complaints on numerous bulletin boards, chat threads or weblogs. She can form alliances and instant pressure groups if she feels a newspaper is being unfair or unbalanced.

The German writer Walter Benjamin predicted this shifting relationship between writer and reader as far back as 1936. He wrote: 'It began with the daily press opening to its readers space for "letters to the editor". And today there is hardly a gainfully employed European who could not, in principle, find an opportunity to publish somewhere or other comments on his work, grievances, documentary reports, or that sort of thing. Thus, the distinction between author and public is about to lose its basic character.'

In the past 10 years or so the process has accelerated. Some newspapers are in denial about this dramatic shift. But most journalists can sense this change, and the smart ones welcome it.

They know that whatever the subject – Israel, hunting, animal rights, GM crops, the euro, drugs – every word they write is going to bounce around the world to be scrutinised, picked over, contested and rebutted. If they get something wrong someone, somewhere, is going to pick up on it. In future, it is going to be much harder for newspapers to play fast and loose with facts or to be wildly unbalanced in their comment.

That is the new world, some would say at its most negative, but there are positive benefits for journalists. They are now permanently plugged into a resource far wider and more knowledgeable than that narrow pinnacle of informed sources on which they used to rely. Smart journalists are learning to use the resource. They can test what Whitehall or Westminster is telling them against the reality in the classroom, the hospital ward or on the railways. They can echo David Mamet on the theatre: 'I've never met an audience that wasn't collectively smarter than I am, and didn't beat me to the punch every time.'

That is the overall context in which this second collection of Corrections and Clarifications appears. The role of Guardian readers' editor is a recognition of the way the world has changed. Newspapers are no longer tablets of stone passed down to the grateful reader. They are much more like a two-way conversation.

At its most basic, we correct mistakes, big and small. It is now impossible to imagine the Guardian ever abandoning this most fundamental daily duty. If readers don't trust a newspaper to get things right – and to correct things when it gets them wrong – they will turn elsewhere for their news. It's that simple.

This aspect of the readers' editor's job recently received important backing in the High Court when a judge capped the libel damages a plaintiff could claim from the Guardian because we had readily agreed to publish a correction and apology, which the plaintiff had spurned. Mr Justice Morland said Ian Mayes had acted 'honourably, independently and competently'.

This was a significant precedent which might encourage other newspapers to consider setting up their own equivalent of the system we have run at the Guardian for the past five years.

The other part of the job – clarifying – is also one which has developed during Ian's time, and which will continue to develop. Bill Kovach and Tom Rosenstiel, two of the most thoughtful American press commentators (one a former ombudsman), recently wrote of this process:

'The individual reporter may not be able to move much beyond a surface level of accuracy in a first story. But the first story builds to a second, in which the sources of news have responded to mistakes and missing elements in the first, and the second to the third and so on. Context is added in each successive layer. In more important and complex stories, there are subsequent contributions on the editorial pages, the talk shows, in the op-ed accounts, and the letters to the editor or the callers to the radio shows – the full range of public and private conversation. This practical truth is a protean thing which, like learning, grows as a stalagmite in a cave, drop by drop over time.' (*The Elements of Journalism*, Random House, 2001)

As Kovach and Rosenstiel imply, this process of adding nuance, detail and context, does not usually occur within the context of a Corrections and Clarifications column. On a running story, the new material may simply accumulate day by day in the news and comment pages. But the corrections column is an acknowledgment of this process and it is useful – and sometimes important – to have an independent figure within a paper who can act as a conduit of views and as a disinterested arbiter in areas of dispute. Journalism is a blunt instrument.

Ian Mayes created the role on the Guardian – the first such Readers' editor in Britain – and three other national newspapers now have something similar. Some of them are members of an international body the Organisation of News Ombudsmen, which is dedicated to the principle to which the Guardian subscribes – that journalists should be accountable for what they do.

The ombudsmen are worth listening to because their daily lives involve much closer contact with readers and with the subjects of stories than any editor can manage. They soon become aware of a) the effect even slight errors, slips of taste or invasions of privacy can have on people's lives, and b) that pinpointing the truth is a difficult, if not impossible, task for busy, time-pressed journalists working in not very open societies. Every newspaper should have one.

Introduction

Ian Mayes

This is the second collection of corrections and columns to come out of my work as readers' editor of the Guardian and it coincides, more or less, with the completion of five years in the job. I have to say, as I did on the first occasion, that the corrections are just the lighter, and perhaps funnier, ones. The serious ones – the real concern of the column – are for fairly obvious reasons not here. On the daily page they run together, but always with the more serious ones first. Most people – not quite all – accept this as sufficient indication that we recognise the distinction. We do and we trust readers to do the same.

My Open Door columns mainly fall into three categories: those discussing ethical issues raised by Guardian journalism; those in which the workings of the Guardian are described; and articles in which the Guardian's endlessly entertaining use and misuse of the English language are discussed. I dealt in the earlier book – rather unsuccessfully as it turns out – with the paper's tiresome use of bad language. There is a fourth category comprising a small number of columns which in themselves constitute corrections. Examples of that kind here are one devoted to the question: Was Billy the Kid left-handed? (the answer is, as an authoritative reader suggested, no); and another that addressed the question: Was a pool player who called himself Fast Eddie Parker (the subject of a Guardian obituary) the model for Fast Eddie Felson, the part played by Paul Newman in the film, The Hustler? Eleonora Tevis, whose late husband Walter Tevis wrote the novel, The Hustler, argued successfully, as you will see, that the answer to this was no too. Mrs Tevis was so delighted to set the record straight after years of struggle with various claimants and newspapers that we had a night out on the town in New York and dinner in the Algonquin.

That was in the spring of 2001, the year in which, later on, New York and the world changed. I have included the columns that discuss or sometimes anticipate readers' questions about the way the paper responded to the events of September 11 – and indeed continues to respond. I have also included three articles in which I discuss charges that in the context of the Israeli-Palestinian conflict the paper had been anti-semitic – a discussion which had to take place under a barrage of emails from adversarial international lobbies. All of this has reinforced my belief in the virtue of the open platform the Guardian provides and in the principle of accountability, even though I have sometimes felt like the man with the whistle trying to referee a very rough game. The tone we should aim to achieve in correspondence between the newspaper and its readers is that of a civilised conversation. Most of the time we come close, even when disagreeing.

A portion of my royalties from this book I am donating to a cause close to my heart, the William Hazlitt Memorial Fund, the main purpose of which is to restore Hazlitt's grave in St Anne's churchyard, Soho, London. Much of the money so far has been raised by public subscription, mainly from readers of the Guardian. Hazlitt himself has provided a stimulus by standing in for me as the posthumous author of the Open Door column on several occasions when I have been on holiday, and an edited extract from one of his essays has appeared.

I have to acknowledge help from a large number of people. My present assistant Helen Hodgson; Murray Armstrong, Barbara Harper, Leslie Plommer, John Cunningham, who have all done stints as readers' editor in my absence; my former assistants Kate McLaughlin, Rose de Paeztron, and Caroline Furneaux; and among colleagues in the 'bunker', Wendy Collinson, the personal assistant to the managing editor, Chris Elliott; Margaret Busby for friendly counsel and for compiling the index; and my publisher at the Guardian, Lisa Darnell.

My colleagues at the Guardian have – readers of the daily catalogue of horrors, rather than the light selection here, may be surprised to know – given a fairly convincing impression of support.

Finally, I would like to thank the readers, a great many of whom have shown themselves to be perfectly reasonable.

→ (more) COR
REC-
TIONS &
→ Clarific
-ations
~~two~~

Corrections & Clarifications

<u>Open Door</u>
<u>July 2000</u> → July 2002

What's in a title?: a brief restatement of intent
→ 19 January 2002

Perhaps it is time to explain myself again and tell you, or remind you, what it is that I am attempting to do. I am prompted by the frequency with which I am still asked, 'What is a readers' editor?' – a question that persists even though I have been doing the job for more than four years and despite the fact that three other British newspapers (the Observer, the Mirror and the Independent on Sunday) now have readers' editors too.

I am not surprised by the question. The paper acquires new readers, and readers who have been with the paper for years often tread well-worn paths without noticing what is going on or changing in the rest of the paper. But journalists, too, are not always clear about my role. Bemused expressions among more recent arrivals sometimes remind me that, when I started the job at the end of 1997, there were fewer than 250 staff journalists on the paper, and there are now more than 350.

The brief answer to the question is that the readers' editor is the independent internal ombudsman of the Guardian. It is a full-time job conducted from a room – a glass box – on the main news floor of the paper in a cluster of offices known (ironically perhaps) as the Bunker, at the centre of which is the editor of the paper. Setting up the role was his idea, as an exercise in self-regulation providing greater access and accountability, and, it was hoped, increasing the bond of trust between the paper and its readers.

The first paragraph of my terms of reference charges me 'to collect, consider, investigate, respond to, and where appropriate come to a conclusion about readers' comments, concerns, and complaints in a prompt and timely manner, from a position of independence within the paper'.

The 'independence' is something I am always questioned about. How can you be paid by the Guardian and at the same time investigate complaints against it independently? It is true that I am paid by the Guardian, no longer as a member of its staff but on a two-year contract. My independence is underwritten by a number of clauses in the terms of reference. For example, the paragraph requiring me to write this weekly column says, 'The content to be determined independently and not subject to prior approval by the editor or others on his staff.'

The terms also say that 'the readers' editor should have an established right of access to the editor, to heads of department meetings, budget meetings, to daily news conferences, and to other relevant forums'. And most importantly, so far as independence is concerned, they say that the readers' editor can only be removed from the post [within the term of a contract] by a vote of the Scott Trust, which owns the Guardian, and of which, it has to be said, the editor is an influential member.

In fact, I have felt able to act in a completely independent manner, and any inadequacies in the service are due more to the volume of complaints or other queries with which I and my assistant, Helen Hodgson, are asked to deal. I am well aware, more so than anyone, of the number of complaints and calls for correction that do not get answered. I can only point to the daily corrections and clarifications column as evidence that we are doing our best, and perhaps invite comparison with the practice of most other newspapers.

But, to return to the question of independence. In four years the editor has on no occasion tried to veto the subject of one of these Open Door columns, nor to interfere with its content. Neither has he vetoed or prevented the publication of any correction or apology that I have deemed it necessary to carry in the daily corrections and clarifications column which I edit, and usually write, on the leader page of the paper, although he retains the right to be consulted about entries in that column.

If a journalist seems unprepared to help with an inquiry, then I can under my terms of reference 'require of the editor that he take steps to ensure that his staff cooperate fully and promptly'. I cannot recall ever invoking this provision. It is rarely a problem. One of the truly encouraging things about doing the job at the Guardian is the more or less general commitment to the principles involved. Indeed, it is common for journalists who become aware of an error in something they have written to tell me about it and ask for a correction to be carried.

The overall intention is that the role should make a positive rather than negative contribution to the Guardian in its various manifestations, and that I should, for instance, 'seek to ensure the maintenance of high standards of accuracy, fairness and balance in our reporting and writing' and encourage 'greater responsiveness to readers'. Yes, I know there is a long way to go.

Bond of trust: the Guardian's new editorial code
→ 02 February 2002

From this week the Guardian publishes its editorial code on its website for all to see, and perhaps, as a colleague said, for some of you 'to beat us with'. It is the first newspaper in Britain to do this and it joins a select group of media organisations, mostly newspapers, around the world prepared to declare the standards to which they aspire and by which they are prepared to be judged.

It is not a code of conduct that requires the raising of the right hand and the swearing of an oath of allegiance. It is not a set of restrictions that will hamper the pursuit of vigorous or investigative journalism. It is a set of guidelines that covers both professional practice and personal behaviour where the latter involves, or might be considered to involve a conflict of interest. It is intended to reinforce the paper's commitment to openness and accountability.

It represents, if you like, an attempt to set down what the Guardian thinks you, its readers, expect of its staff journalists and the freelances who write for it. It incorporates a good many points that you have raised in your complaints and comments to me and my colleagues over the past few years. It is in part, therefore, a code that, imperfect and incomplete though we shall almost certainly discover it to be, expresses the paper's relationship with its readers.

To begin at the beginning, let me quote from the preamble to the code. It starts, in fact, with a quotation from the Guardian's most famous editor, CP Scott: 'A newspaper's primary office is the gathering of news. At the peril of its soul it must see that the supply is not tainted.' (The whole of the article that Scott wrote to mark the centenary of the Guardian in 1921 is given as an appendix to the code. This is the article in which he says, 'Comment is free, but facts are sacred.')

The voice of the present editor may be recognised in what follows: 'The most important currency of the Guardian is trust. . . . The purpose of this code is, above all, to protect and foster the bond of trust between the paper and its readers, and therefore to protect the integrity of the paper and of the editorial content it carries.'

It continues with a sentence that represents the resolution of discussions with the journalists' union: 'As a set of guidelines, this will not form part of a journalist's contract of employment, nor will it form part, for either editorial management or journalists, of disciplinary, promotional or recruitment procedures.' This reflects anxieties over provisions, to some extent amended, which it was felt would inhibit extramural, particularly political, activities of the paper's journalists. It means that the code as it is now worded relies on commitment not by edict but by the power of its contents to persuade reasonable minds. That seems to me to be fair enough.

As the preamble says: '. . . by observing the code, journalists working for the Guardian will be protecting not only the paper but also the independence, standing and reputation of themselves and their colleagues. It is important that freelances working for the Guardian also abide by these guidelines while on assignment for the paper.'

What is written into the terms of employment for Guardian journalists is a requirement to adhere to the code of conduct of the press Complaints Commission, the PCC, the full text of which is also attached to the Guardian code as an appendix. Why, you may wonder, if you have the PCC code (there is also a National Union of Journalists' code), do you need another? Perusal of the Guardian's code, which uses asterisks to refer readers to relevant sections of the PCC code, will quickly demonstrate that the Guardian code is much more wide-ranging and specific to its own practice.

The editor of the Guardian sees the formulation and publication of the code as a natural development after introducing the role of readers' editor: 'You are saying that your relationship with readers matters and that you are committed to accountability and transparency.' On outside activities, he said it was intended to alert journalists at least to the possibility of conflicts of interest that might cause the paper's transparency to be questioned.

The code would have the practical purpose of providing in one place the Guardian's statement of policy on a wide variety of matters, for example on errors, invective, plagiarism, race, freebies and the declaration of sources.

Interest free?: the importance of accountability
→ 09 February 2002

The Wall Street Journal announced this week, in a leader headed Scribbler's Ethics, that Professor Roger Scruton would not be writing for it again – or, as the paper put it, 'he will be taking a holiday from our pages' – because he failed to declare a relevant interest. He wrote for it on tobacco issues without revealing that he was being paid a retainer by a major tobacco company, a connection that the Guardian subsequently made public.

His banishment was noted in the Guardian's City diary on Wednesday this week. However, the Guardian does not have an unblemished record in this respect. It has also on several occasions in the past few years published material without declaring a relevant interest, either because the author had withheld it or because the commissioning editor did not consider it something that readers need be told. My advice, when there is doubt whether disclosure of an interest is necessary, is to give the reader the benefit of the doubt and declare it. Writers should always inform the editor for whom they are working of any interest they think should be declared.

The Wall Street Journal in its editorial said, 'Our own view is that the financing of the advocate matters far less than the quality of the advocacy. But our longtime standard is also that such financial ties should be disclosed, so that readers can make up their own minds.'

This is, in part, what the Guardian code says: 'It is always necessary to declare an interest when the journalist is writing about something with which he or she has a significant connection. This applies to both staff journalists and freelances writing for the Guardian. The declaration should be to a head of department or editor during preparation. Full transparency may mean that the declaration should appear in the paper or website as well.'

In some circumstances the declaration of interest is, in effect, a declaration of the writer's qualifications for writing the piece. As the code says, 'Some connections are obvious and represent the reason why the writer has been asked to contribute to the paper. These should always be stated at the end of the writer's contribution, even if he or she contributes regularly, so long as the writer is writing about his or her area of interest.'

Doing this is one of the things that makes new readers feel welcome. It is all very well to say, as the Wall Street Journal is saying, that it is 'the quality of the advocacy' that counts. I hear it quite often put a different way – surely it is the argument we should be concentrating on rather than the credentials of the author. We can agree with all that, but newspaper readers have, or should have, a healthy scepticism that will not be dispelled by the discovery afterwards of something they should have been told before.

The most controversial part of the new code is, or was, while it was being negotiated, the section dealing with the outside interests and activities of the paper's staff journalists and the freelances who contribute regularly to it, particularly those who appear so frequently that they are closely identified with the Guardian.

Some journalists saw this as a possible restriction of their freedom, especially of their political freedom. All that this part of the code does, however, is to urge an open relationship with the reader. If a journalist has not declared an interest, and I will outline some of the circumstances in which he or she might be expected to do that in a moment, then the reader has the right to expect that the writer is unencumbered or untrammelled by unstated ties or allegiances.

This is what the code actually says: 'Guardian staff journalists should be sensitive to the possibility that activities outside work (including holding office or being otherwise actively involved in organisations, companies or political parties) could be perceived as having a bearing on – or as coming into conflict with – the integrity of our journalism.

'Staff should be transparent about any outside personal, philosophical or financial interests which might conflict with their professional performance of duties at the Guardian, or could be perceived to do so.' The advice here is: when in doubt, discuss it with the editor.

I once worked for an editor who, on his retirement, revealed that he belonged to – was involved in – no fewer than 37 organisations in the town where we published. The present executive editor of the Washington Post is so keen to maintain an unimpeachable independence that he has said he does not exercise his right to vote. Most of us are located within this scale and have no interest in keeping anything from you.

Press charges: newspapers and accountability
→ 02 December 2000

Here are two questions that have cropped up rather more often than usual in the past week. Why are newspapers, which are constantly calling for accountability in others, generally so reluctant to be accountable themselves? What possible reason could a newspaper, or a newspaper's website, have for declining to correct some significant thing it had got wrong?

As a matter of fact, I have been putting these questions myself in reply to questions put to me as I have gone round publicising the first collection of these Saturday columns and the Guardian's (funnier) corrections.

The questions I have been asked most frequently are, 'Why does the Guardian run daily corrections?', usually coupled with 'Is it because it makes more mistakes than anyone else?' and 'Why don't the other papers carry regular corrections?' This last question is usually coupled with another, 'Is it because they never, or hardly ever, make mistakes?'

I cannot answer for other papers and we have no way of knowing whether the Guardian makes more mistakes than others, but I would certainly look more than a little sceptically at a journalist who stood up to declare, 'We never make mistakes.' You may take it as read that they all do.

The editor of the Guardian, writing a diary in this week's New Statesman, notes the advent of a readers' editor, modelled on the Guardian system, at Politiken, the Danish newspaper, then adds, 'But so far, one has to confess, the idea has not spread like a bushfire through the British press.*

'Do other editors really believe their readers will trust them less if they keep admitting they got things wrong? Can't they see that the reverse is true?

It certainly is true to say that an increasing number of journalists on other papers are making it clear that they would welcome a franker relationship of this kind with their readers. The Express, for example, in mentioning the book, said that, 'Since its introduction as "a forum for accountability" in 1997, [the Guardian's corrections system] has been an unqualified success.' A senior journalist on the Express, in a radio discussion a week ago, said, '. . . it is utterly proper that if you get something wrong, you should correct it at the first possible opportunity and not try and squabble'.

In the same programme (Radio 5 Live's Paper Talk, presented by Brian Hayes on November 24), a senior journalist from the Telegraph said – and we must take it that he was speaking generally and not with specific reference to his own paper – 'I think one of the most disgraceful things about our business is our refusal actually to admit when we get things wrong. And as newspaper journalists we're brought up – and it certainly happened to me – to do everything we can to avoid apologising or issuing a correction. . . .

'We spend hours trying to persuade people who have every reason to expect a correction, will they accept a letter from us saying "I'm sorry we got this wrong"? And when they say "Well, no, we want a correction in the paper", [we say] "Well would you write a letter to the paper?"'

'I don't know why we do it, because the Guardian, I think, is doing brilliantly with this system.'

Clive Soley, the chairman of the Parliamentary Labour party and joint author of Regulating The Press (published by Pluto), lamented in a recent article in the Times, 'The press is very reluctant either to say sorry – most don't even have a correction column – or to admit that they got it wrong.'

A senior journalist on the Times, reviewing the Guardian's [first] Corrections book, shares some of our best or worst moments with his readers but points out, 'The truth is that similar cock-ups appear in most newspapers most days . . . If a newspaper is prepared to admit to error. . . it establishes a relationship of trust with readers for being honest enough to admit mistakes.'

When I talked to postgraduate journalism students at the City University in London this week, I fancied I detected a flicker of surprise and dismay when I said that society at large did not hold the journalist in high esteem. A more open and mature relationship is in everyone's interest, and maybe the students from the City, and others just entering the profession, will do something to foster it.

A willingness to correct things when you know they are wrong does not seem too much to ask. Why, perhaps we shall soon be asking, did it take us all so long to get round to it?

* Since this column was written, the Observer,
the Mirror and the Independent on Sunday
have all appointed readers' editors

Shades of doubt: why common errors are no less wrong
→ 09 September 200

No part of the paper escapes the scrutiny of readers, but some parts are scrutinised more than others. Among these are the leader columns where, recently, we wrote, 'Youngsters are undoubtably inspired by the Ginolas and Zolas flaunting their rare skills. . . .' This brought the following email from a reader in Perugia: 'Admittably,' he wrote, 'I have been absent from Britain for over 20 years, but I still find the neologism "undoubtably" somewhat objectionable.' In fact, although 'admittably' may be a neologism, a new word, used here ironically of course, 'undoubtably' undoubtedly is not. It is the opposite, an archaism that seems to have enjoyed a sparse and fairly brief currency during the 15th and early 16th centuries before falling into desuetude (a word that you do not hear very often), if not quite into obsolescence. The Oxford English Dictionary notes it as '? Obs'.

'Undoubtably' had, according to the OED, exactly the same meaning as 'undoubtedly' – the word which has proved to be much more durable and the one which the leader writer undoubtedly intended to use – 'without doubt, indubitably'. The use of 'undoubtably' today is, paradoxically, an error but not an inaccuracy.

It would be nice to think that its use was conscious and that we were deliberately led into a surprising encounter with it in the flat linguistic terrain of contemporary daily journalism. I am afraid not. It is a common and unwitting substitute, particularly perhaps in speech, for the word that enjoys the approved status.

It is difficult to say whether it is, or is about to become, one of those errors so commonly used that it ceases to be regarded as an error and instead gains first our tolerance and then our acceptance as a legitimate part of the language. I think not – not, at any rate, in the foreseeable future. It does not appear in Collins Millennium edition, which has an ear for changes, an absence that may reassure the expatriate (not ex-patriot, as we have been known to say) in Perugia. Nevertheless, its history is seductive and even though it is always these days used in ignorance, and we should disapprove of it, I am not actually affronted by it.

Readers point out other things, often far more irritating, which appear to fall into the same category of ignorant use bringing pressure to bear for change through persistence and proliferation. The confusion of singular and plural is an example and we are guilty of this in many ways.

One of them was illustrated by a headline not long ago in which we said, 'President Putin needs time and money to steer his country's transition to a market economy. And neither are in very great supply.' We should have said, 'And neither is in very great supply' – neither one nor the other is . . .

On this point Collins is clear, offering the following guidance on usage after its definition of neither: 'A verb following a compound subject that uses neither . . . (nor) should be in the singular if both subjects are in the singular: neither Jack nor John has done the work.'

The New Fowler's Modern English usage is good on this, pointing out exceptions and complications, for instance when both subjects are not singular: 'Neither eyes nor nose (does its, do their) work' – a complication arising from the use of eyes, plural, with nose, singular.

The current edition of Fowler retains the following admirable advice from the 1926 edition: 'The wise man, in writing, evades these problems by rejecting the alternatives – any of which may set up friction between him and his reader – and putting the thing in some other shape.' (The wise man today would avoid a sentence as resoundingly masculine as that – something guaranteed to set up friction.)

The use of 'none', over which we often stumble, is much more straightforward and should almost always be followed by a singular form of verb: but then none of us is perfect.

Readers like to feel that we are at least aspiring to meticulous accuracy ('meticulous inaccuracy' was Proust's satirical comment on the writings of the Goncourt brothers) in our use of the language. A doctor wrote recently to comment on the following statement by another doctor in G2: 'I have delivered babies to single mothers.' This was not an unusual error, he said, 'but it should really have been "I have delivered single mothers" or "I have delivered single mothers of their babies."' He added, 'It is a nice point, I know, but it is storks, rather than doctors, that deliver babies.' He is right, of course.

Sometimes our informality (a word which Fowler sees as code for 'illiterate', 'vulgar' or 'sloppy') goes too far. We recently noticed a motorist who was 'sat in a queue' and a person who 'promised to work for free'. A little loose, perhaps, even by our standards.

The Proust remark is quoted in Marcel Proust:
A Biography by Jean-Yves Tadié,
tr Euan Cameron (Viking).

A bit of lit crit: a literal misuse of the language
→ 23 September 2000

It is not a good idea to take too literally every word you read in the Guardian. One of the words that are not to be taken too literally is 'literally', the use and abuse of which a reader drew to my attention this week. It did not take long to find examples that are, well, quite literally mind-boggling. Just in the past two or three weeks we have told you that a search party was 'literally heading for a cross on a map', that the world for one poor individual had 'literally gone pear-shaped', and that 'the pizza business in Britain is literally taking off'. This last one was a reference to the Russian Proton rocket which made its journey to the International Space Station this summer with a Pizza Hut logo on its side. Literally, a rocket took off with a logo on the side. Figuratively the pizza business took off too.

Most of the guides to good English have something to say about 'literally'. The Teach Yourself Concise Dictionary of Correct English, for example, reminds us of the rigour of the literal definition. 'Literally means "exactly in accordance with the meaning of the word(s)" to which "literally" is attached.'

The author of this book, BA Phythian, by way of illustration, says it is only acceptable to say that a thief was literally caught red-handed if he had red hands. Literally, Phythian says, is often wrongly used in this way, merely as a means of emphasis, with some ridiculous consequences, 'The players literally ran out of steam.'

Godfrey Howard, in The Macmillan Good English Handbook, takes a more relaxed view. He says, 'If a knife is literally as sharp as a razor, it should be possible to shave with it. But literally is so often used to mean, not in reality but in a manner of speaking: "dinner at that restaurant literally costs the earth".'

He adds, 'This use of "literally" is far too common to make a fuss about it, but we might prefer to be careful ourselves to use "literally" only when we mean in reality.' One of the things for the writer to consider, he suggests, is whether the word could be left out altogether.

The best piece of advice, I think, is that given in The New Fowler's Modern English usage, but we shall come to that in a moment. The reader who (literally) started this train of thought, enclosed two extracts from the autobiography of the author Compton Mackenzie, who revealed in a letter to the Evening Standard in about 1928, 'An amusement of mine for many years has been collecting "literallys"' (My Life and Times, Octave 6, 1923-30).

Sir Compton offered a few items from his collection, including one from the Evening Standard itself 'when a distinguished Admiral was said to have literally won his spurs at the Battle of Jutland', and another, from a court report in which the accused was said to have 'literally gone to pieces after his arrest'.

He concluded his letter to the Standard, 'As I write these words I hear on the Wireless from Mr PF Warner that WG Grace "literally" killed the fast bowlers of the last century, which must have kept his brother EM, the coroner, fairly busy' (ah, my Warner and my Grace, long ago).

Mackenzie thought it was much too kind to the culprits to excuse them simply for mistaking 'literally' with 'figuratively'. 'Are they not looking for one of those wretched augmentatives which, like inflated tics, batten on the language?' – an augmentative in this sense being a word whose purpose is to emphasise or reinforce the word or phrase to which it is attached. So 'literally' sacrifices its own true meaning to lend its weight to all manner of outrageous statements.

The results, as we have seen are often so amusing that it seems a bit churlish to complain. We do not want to be spoilsports, do we? We knew exactly what Bel Littlejohn, a famously forthright columnist, meant when she wrote in her own vivid way, 'I went into Melvyn's office unannounced and found him ... sitting beneath a literally shattering new piece by Damien Hirst.'

The reader, who raised 'literally', by the way, also suggested that it had been joined by 'famously' as what he called 'the wretched augmentative of 2000'. He quoted from our recent rerun of the Lady Chatterley trial when the prosecution counsel 'famously' asked the jury, 'Is it a book you would wish your wife or servants to read?' On Monday this week we used 'famously' in 10 separate pieces, certainly qualifying the word as a cliche.

Now, the final word on 'literally' from the New Fowler, which after an example from the Guardian, 1995, 'They [the supermarkets] can literally play God, even to the point of sending food back to the genetic drawing board for a redesign, 'concludes its discussion with the following words of advice, 'It's a case of "stop, look and think" before using the word in any manner short of its exact sense.'

Precisely. Do that and we shall get along famously.

Dead reckoning: using pictures of the boy shot in Gaza
→ 07 October 2000

On Tuesday this week the lead story in our tabloid second section, G2, was about the shooting in Gaza of the 12-year-old Palestinian boy, Mohammed al-Durrah. It was illustrated with all but one of the eight available frames showing the last moments of the boy's life, filmed by a Palestinian cameraman working for French television.

These images were shown on television on Saturday night. Two of the frames appeared on the front page of late editions of the Observer, the only paper to use them so prominently on Sunday – something for which several of the paper's readers criticised it (in my view misguidedly, or let us say precipitately, since I believe that the events of the week have endorsed the decision to use the pictures).

I inquired about the reaction from Observer readers to see whether it had differed in any way from the response to the Guardian's use of these images. On almost every occasion in the past three years when we have used pictures as strong as these, and certainly when we have shown pictures of dead people – in Northern Ireland, Kosovo, Sierra Leone or Zimbabwe – a number of you have complained, and on all of those occasions we have considered the pros and cons in this column. This time, by Thursday anyway, many of you had voiced your reaction to the event, and a selection of your letters was published, but no one complained that our use of the pictures was intrusive, exploitative, cynical or sensational, the accusations made on previous occasions. Did we do something right?

By the time the Guardian used the pictures on Tuesday it seems likely that most of the paper's readers had seen some of them already. By Tuesday our website had considered and rejected the idea of putting up the movie footage, I think rightly, although one of the senior journalists involved in our treatment of the story in the paper said he could not see any distinction in ethical terms between showing still pictures (which we did) and moving pictures (which we did not). Can you?

Our Middle East editor has written about this in his column on our website. For those of you who do not have internet access, this is what he says: 'Inevitably, video clips have appeared on the internet and now all you need do is click your mouse to have Mohammed brought back to life and shot again and again and again. Apart from being unbelievably ghoulish, this removes the event from the brutal realities of Middle East politics and dumps it in the realm of fantasy video games.'

Let us turn back to G2. The front page was stripped of the contents panel that normally runs across the top of the page and instead the contents were flagged in a single line across the foot of the page. This released almost the whole of the page for an image of the terrified Mohammed sheltering beneath the protective arm of his father. It carried the headline: What really happened at Netzarim crossroads?

The following three pages, which included six more of the images from the sequence, sought an answer. Our correspondent went to the scene, spoke to the cameraman, and interviewed the boy's mother and others in a straightforward and memorable piece of reporting that suggested that the boy and his father had been targeted and shot by Israeli soldiers. The Israeli authorities have since said the two were mistaken for gunmen.

The deputy editor (news) said that looking at the situation on Monday he felt that what was needed was a piece of reporting to try to cut through the obfuscation that was then prevalent. The presentation was obviously shocking but not gratuitously so. 'For all sorts of reasons you wanted to know exactly what had happened. The boy and his father were there for something like 45 minutes. You felt indignation. And the internal reaction, the reaction inside Israel – 21 lines in the main paper – was past understanding.'

The editor of G2 said the image on the front on Tuesday would radicalise you. 'It would make you want to pick up a stone.' But he said his main anxiety was not to act as judge and jury. If it was a trial you would want more evidence than we had been able to produce, good though it was.

I asked the journalist who wrote the report what effect she thought the pictures had had. She said inside the country they had hardened the hearts of Israelis and made the Palestinians more violent. She felt that more rather than fewer people had died as an immediate result.

Farther away, we hope they have a different effect. Someone in the office said, 'You immediately think of the child closest to you, whether you have children of your own or not.' You want it to stop. In passing we might ask ourselves what we know about the other children, one of them only two years old, who have died in the violence this week.

Missive attack: personal correspondence
→ 14 Oct 2000

Most Guardian writers now seem to accept, with some reservations, that it is a positively good thing that their readers should have direct access to them through email. Published pieces carrying an email address attract at least four or five letters to the writer. Fifteen is quite common, and a particularly controversial piece may bring in, say, 40.

Now, with the contents of the paper available on the website, and Guardian journalists being commissioned increasingly to write new material directly for the website, responses may come from anywhere in the world. Email encourages this easy correspondence. All the journalists I have spoken to this week say they get far more reaction to their work by email than they ever received by conventional post which now, in all cases, accounts for only a minority of letters received.

The email correspondence tends to be more relaxed in tone. Several writers mentioned the marked difference they had observed in email sent directly to them and the correspondence about their work published on the letters page. Mail to the writer often said nice things about the article, or offered the writer useful additional information, or the addresses of organisations or individuals relevant to the subject of the piece. One or two journalists said they had developed a genuinely useful relationship with email correspondents.

How much reader-to-writer email gets answered is practically impossible to tell. One writer said, 'I'm always behind answering my email but I am quite diligent in responding and in the end everyone gets a reply. On the first day back in the office after a couple of weeks away I spend the whole day answering the email.'

Email exchanges between reader and writer must already account for a significant volume of correspondence. Several writers questioned whether this might in the long term pose a threat to the letters page, the real public forum. The letters page is very highly valued both inside and outside the paper. It receives, now mainly by email of course, almost 100,000 letters a year of which 6 percent or 7 percent are published, about one in 16. The huge oversubscription of the letters page obviously feeds its vitality. However, it does mean that in any year there are perhaps 90,000 readers who have suffered the frustration of failing to see their letters in print. The quality of the letters page might well suffer – there is no sign of this at the moment – if large numbers of readers simply decided to settle for private correspondence with the writer.

It is quite important that those of you who are using the opportunity to email journalists directly ask yourselves whether you also want your letter to be considered for publication. If you do, then copy it, to letters@guardian.co.uk or, better, send another version to the letters page. The letters editor says that emails intended for publication are very often, as they need to be, more focused and briefer than the more relaxed and informal mail to the journalist.

I mentioned that there were some reservations. Some journalists felt that the burden on their time, if they answered all their correspondence, was too great and interfered with their 'real work'. Several, particularly those receiving a lot of email, felt that in opening their office email addresses to you, the readers, they had surrendered their own privacy and ran the risk of losing important messages from colleagues, or the email from a partner asking them to pick up a pint of milk on the way home.

Why not, they asked, have a parallel email system so that in-office emails and personal emails could be kept separate? There are practical difficulties in doing that, and to some extent it would work against the idea of direct access and accountability, which is what we are really talking about. I think these reservations will disappear in time. Email can be sifted extremely quickly, and those who receive it must simply answer what they can.

In my experience most people are reasonable about this. The 100,000 letters to the editor received every year are not acknowledged. I reply to most but not all of the correspondence addressed to me as readers' editor, generally hoping that those who see the point they raised dealt with in the corrections and clarifications column will consider that to be sufficient acknowledgment.

I have some sympathy with the desire for a special email network expressed by those colleagues whose work brings hate mail down upon them. If you have never received anything like it you may not understand how disturbing this rubbish can be. Perhaps I should publish a selection some time. But it is not something that should be allowed to stand in our way. As I have said before the correspondence between the newspaper and its readers, in an ideal world, should be a conversation between intelligent friends. That is the way we are going.

Since this article was written the volume of email has increased considerably and a parallel email system has been introduced for some journalists.

As you like it: unfavourable comparisons
→ 21 October 2000

Readers who believe that the Guardian should be written in decent English pursue their cause relentlessly. No feelings of propriety persuade them to withhold their criticism, even from our reporting of disasters. We may be recounting the most shocking events in the world, but we shall still not be spared the insistent finger pointing to the grammatical lapse. Its discovery distracts the mind of this type of reader (a type to which I probably belong) from the actual content, no matter how serious that is.

Readers who have this condition in its advanced stages not only notice the particular thing that annoys them whenever it occurs. They notice it, with a little leap of delight, when it does not occur but might have done. One of them, as a matter of fact, sent me a message this week beginning, 'Congratulations to the Guardian for printing "as if" (October 18, page 3, col 2) [in place of "like"].' This related to a quoted sentence from one of the survivors of the Hatfield rail crash: 'The roof of one carriage had been peeled off as if it was a sardine can.'

Did this mean, the reader wondered, that 'like' was irritatingly used instead of 'as if' only when we were not quoting but using our own words? So it was not a message of congratulation after all – not one, anyway, without a twist of the lip.

Here are a couple of examples that had the inflammatory effect, both from recent pieces in the Guardian, where 'as if' or 'as though' should have been used. 'A lot of the time, she looks quite scared, like she has seen a freakishly large spider in the bath' 'It looks like [football] "fans" with no previous form are the problem this week.'

Readers get just as worked up when we use 'like' to mean 'such as', perhaps even more prevalent. Here's a letter from a reader of Guardian Europe: 'Almost every day I read stories in the Guardian containing the word "like" (in the meaning of "similar") when the writer should be using "such as".' He quoted as an example a fairly recent front-page story about football transfer fees in which we said, 'Players like Manchester United's David Beckham and Roy Keane, as well as other high-profile footballers, stand to benefit.'

'Surely,' this reader asked, '[this] reads better as "Players such as Manchester United's David Beckham and Roy Keane stand to benefit".'

One reader complaining about 'like' for 'as if' commented, 'I don't know whether this is allowed in your style guide. I rather hope not for me it strikes a particularly jarring note.' The reader goes on to say, 'Your general policy of adapting to change, but not too fast, must be right.'

There is a struggle in progress over all these constructions. Collins, the dictionary to which we turn only for points not covered in our house style guide, includes the 'non-standard' use of like as a conjunction meaning 'as though [or] as if' as its seventh definition of the word, with the example, 'You look like you've just seen a ghost.' However, in its note on usage, it says, 'The use of like to mean such as was formerly thought to be undesirable in formal writing, but has now become acceptable.'

Mr Burchfield, the editor of The New Fowler's Modern English Usage, whom I often quote on such matters, runs nimbly over the ground and concludes, 'It would appear that in many kinds of written and spoken English, like as a conjunction is struggling towards acceptable standard or neutral ground. It is not there yet.' But it is, he suggests, only a matter of time. On the question of like meaning such as, Fowler seems to be suggesting it is six of one and half a dozen of the other.

We would be deprived of all this innocent amusement if those who wrote for the Guardian did what they were required to do and followed the style guide. This is what it says: 'Like/as if: never use the former to mean the latter: "it looks as if he's finished", not "it looks like he's finished".'

'Like/such as: like excludes such as includes. "Cities like Manchester are wonderful" suggests that the writer has in mind, say, Sheffield or Birmingham she actually means "Cities such as Manchester".'

Subeditors would be perfectly justified, therefore, in changing the constructions of which readers complain, in line with the authority of the paper's own style guide. The style guide has no authority at all if it is not referred to and its decisions are not implemented.

Many of those who object to the things we have been discussing do so because they see them as Americanisms or American usages. One such reader wrote, 'Recently I saw "trashed" in an otherwise excellent front-page lead story. What is wrong with "destroyed"? Why use "totalled" where "written off" is our expression, and why "car wreck" when the UK expression is "car crash"?'

Some of this is brutalism and it should not require a style guide to keep it out of the paper, unless we are quoting someone, like we do.

Old prejudices: how the language of ageism prevails
→ 06 January 2001

A leader in the Guardian a couple of weeks before Christmas commented on the changing age profile of the population in Britain and other
developed countries. It said: 'We already live in the oldest society that
has existed, but it is going to get older still. Fewer births and longer lives
mean the number of people aged 65 and over will increase at 10 times
the overall rate of population growth in the next 40 years.'

There is still perhaps more awareness of this in the US than in
Britain. A cartoon in the New Yorker in the summer of last year had a
woman addressing her husband with the words: 'Good news, honey – 70
is the new 50.' An episode of Frasier, shown on television in Britain a
month later, had Dr Frasier Crane remarking: 'You sound like my father
– a man who believes that burial is a form of age discrimination.'

About one-quarter of the Guardian's readers are over the age of 55,
more or less equivalent to the proportion on other broadsheets, except
for the Daily Telegraph, which has nearly half its readers in that upper-
age band.

The Guardian, like all its rivals, makes great efforts to attract young
people but still attempts, now and again, a conciliatory nod towards its
older readers. Remarkably, in mid-December the paper started a monthly Grandparents page, the advent of which was marked by the editorial
quoted above. The editor of the page, a man some long way from becoming a grandparent, pointed out in a persuasive introductory article that
40 percent of parents admit that their working lives would be impossible without the childcare provided by their own parents. It should be
worth watching the page as it explores the implications of that and other
aspects of a long life sanctioned by an assumed or assigned role.

My correspondence leaves me in no doubt that many readers, particularly those who are themselves in the upper-age bracket, believe the
paper is at best confused in its attitude to age, and at worst ageist. To
return to the editorial I was quoting, it continued thus: 'The US is
already seeing a rising proportion of wrinklies in work.' (Collins, 'wrinklies': informal, derogatory [term for] old people.)

Several readers combined a welcome for the Grandparents page
with a note of dismay at the use of the word. 'I don't think the word
"wrinkly" is needed in the language, any more than derogatory nicknames for [other groups]. We need to respect all our fellow citizens, not
demean them. Remember what Sophia Loren said about wrinkles: not
to retouch photos showing hers because "it took me so long to earn them".'

Other correspondents made the same point. 'To be defined simply by one aspect of our being – one generally considered negative – is totally out of order and abusively ageist. Shame on the journalist and the editor who passed it.'

In the week before Christmas another piece in the Guardian attracted protest, this time the Diary of a Junior Doctor, in which the author cautioned readers against dumping their 'grannies' in hospital over the festive season.

A letter began: 'I write in some personal distress to protest about an attitude to older people paraded in these columns for the amusement of readers. Try substituting "blacks" or "Jews" for the "grannies" and the piece would have been scrapped on sight.

'And the distress? Well, 35 years ago I changed my medical career to become a full-time advocate for the needs and rights of older people who become sick. At that time attitudes such as these were almost the norm among hospital doctors. It is not pleasant to see such prejudice still in existence and apparently still acceptable enough to be described so shamelessly.'

One reader writing in response, not to this but to another piece, threw in an objection to the way that his or her doctor said: 'You're not 25 any more, you know,' adding: 'But the way doctors treat old people is another story, and a distressing one.' The main purpose of this reader had been to call for the abandonment of the phrase 'the age when men and women pick up their free bus pass', usually used as an oblique compliment to someone still active. 'So and so is starting a new career at the age when...'

This falls into the category of thoughtless ageism like that objected to by the writer of the following letter: 'As a recently diagnosed osteoporosis sufferer, I begin to understand [the] use of the phrase "little old ladies". It is a bad habit grown out of a truism. There are still "little old ladies", but in the past, before diagnosis and treatment of osteoporosis were possible, there must have been many, many more.' It was time, this reader suggested, to stop implying that all old ladies were little.

Times are changing – faster, it sometimes appears, than our language and attitudes. But I'll stop there. It is time for my rest.

The New Yorker cartoon, published in the issue of June 5, last year, was by Victoria Roberts. The episode of Frasier was broadcast in Britain on July 14 last year.

Must do better: a report that makes uncomfortable reading
→ 13 January 2001

We have just completed a rough numerical analysis of entries in our daily Corrections and Clarifications column through one entire year, from November 1999 to the beginning of that month last year. By the time you read this a copy of the results will have been posted on the paper's electronic noticeboard for the examination of all Guardian journalists. I shall tell you about some of the results in a minute, but a few qualifying remarks are necessary.

It is not a league table and there are no gold stars or penalty points. The purpose of the exercise is to provide at least something against which any improvement may be roughly measured in future. The paper is actively seeking to improve its system of checks and to cut down the number of mistakes. Perhaps the figures will stimulate this process, if only because they will stand as a caution against complacency – not that I see much sign of that.

They are, as I say, only a rough guide because, in the first place, not all mistakes come to my notice and not all of those that do are corrected. As a general rule, grammatical errors have been dealt with in clusters in this column on Saturdays rather than in the daily corrections column, although increasingly under pressure from readers to do so, I have been including some of them in the corrections column.

Some of the other, factual, errors escape correction simply because something more important occurs to push them too far down the constantly changing list of priorities. It does not mean that nothing was done: in almost all cases the matter is brought to the attention of the journalist.

Here is one, for example, that did not get into the corrections column. In a front-page report of the appalling fire in Holland on New Year's Eve we referred to the 'inland Ijsselmeer sea'. A reader sent an email from the Hague saying that it is actually a man-made freshwater lake and that it is not spelled Ijsselmeer but IJsselmeer.

The Encarta Online Encyclopedia confirms all this and helpfully points out that one of the rivers from which it receives fresh waters is the IJssel. The reporter was sent a copy of the email. He, in turn, sent an email to the reader pointing out that he had spelled it IJsselmeer but that its double capital letters (representing a single Dutch character) had not survived to reach the printed page (or website). One does not wish to sound like Lady Bracknell, but to have two initial caps must have looked to someone like carelessness.

It is not a matter of huge consequence, although interesting, and of course it is important to get things right. Readers, I have found, do not hesitate to point out this kind of mistake in reports, such as the one in question, of quite horrifying events.

We must keep a sense of proportion, however. Here are the thoughts of Dr Johnson, a familiar figure in this part of London 250 years ago, writing about his friend Richard Savage:

'A superstitious Regard to the Correction of his Sheets was one of Mr Savage's Peculiarities. He often altered, revised, recurred to his first Reading or Punctuation, and again adopted the Alteration. He was dubious and irresolute without End, as on a Question of the last Importance, and at last was seldom satisfied. The Intrusion or Omission of a Comma was sufficient to discompose him, and he would lament an Error of a single Letter as a heavy Calamity.' Johnson, the historian Richard Holmes tells us, 'noted this Quixotic desire for perfect type-setting with shrewd amusement'.

We work in haste and do not, no matter how fretful we may get, have time for that degree of fastidiousness. The figures we have compiled lump all categories of error together and do not differentiate the serious and the less consequential (you may say trivial).

During the year there were almost 1,500 entries in the corrections column, nearly half arising from four main areas. These are pages 1,2 and 3, which are treated as a unit with their own production team (124 corrections); the home news pages, the biggest part of the paper (267) the foreign pages (121), and G2, the tabloid second section (245), excluding the arts pages, the women's, style and parents' pages and the Guide pages with the television programmes, which were all counted separately.

The G2 total, considering it was produced largely by its general feature pages and columns (8,000 to 10,000 words a day), could not be considered good. Not surprisingly the months of August and September, last year, when G2 was understaffed, showed a sharp rise.

Here are the figures for some of the other high-profile sections: the comment and analysis pages, excluding letters, 70; letters, 25; obituaries and birthdays, 79; City 51; sport 74. And yes, sorry, mistakes in corrections: 8.

The analysis of the year's corrections was made by Mary Fitzgerald. The quotation from Dr Johnson comes from his Life of Savage and is quoted in Richard Holmes's Dr Johnson & Mr Savage (Flamingo paperback).

Snap decision: questions raised by pictures of the dead
→ 20 January 2001

Several readers complained about two pictures of dead people published in the Guardian last Tuesday. One appeared on the cover of G2, the tabloid second section of the paper, and the other was carried across pages 2 and 3 of the same issue. Broadly, the complaints were that the pictures were exploitative and intrusive. Three of them came from health service professionals, one a former pathology technician, one a nurse who was on duty at her hospital in Scotland when I spoke to her, and the third a dermatologist.

The cover picture was the one which, in the words of the features editor who took the decision to run it, 'everyone was talking about'. It showed dead bodies lying on the unrefrigerated floor of a chapel in Bedford Hospital. It was used first across the front page of the free newspaper, Bedfordshire on Sunday, whose photographer had taken it, and by the Sunday Telegraph. On Monday it was used in the Mirror and the Daily Mail. The Guardian paid £500 (more than it normally pays for the front of G2) to use it on Tuesday, having been asked initially for £1,500, I was told.

It was used in a medium-sized format, across the equivalent of about three broadsheet columns, floating in the middle of a black front tabloid page carrying these words: 'This photograph has horrified Britain. But what does it tell us more about? The state of the NHS – or the way we feel about death?'

It was a legitimate question to ask and it was intelligently discussed on pages 2 and 3 in an article by the health editor of the paper, a piece described by one of the readers who complained about the accompanying picture as 'informative, balanced and sympathetically written'. That picture showed the feet of a dead man, with a label tied to the big toe of his left foot. In the first edition the writing on the label was clearly visible, dating the picture in 1988, naming the man, giving his address and the cause of death.

Although some of those who complained expressed reservations about the front-page picture, they all objected to this picture on pages 2 and 3. They all lived in parts of Britain which receive early editions of the Guardian.

At about midnight on Monday, the editor of the Guardian saw an early edition, rang the night editor and had the details on the label blurred so that they were illegible for all later editions.

What no one knew at that time was that the photographer had himself changed some of the essential details, including the man's name. The picture was indeed taken in 1988, at a hospital in central London, with the full permission of the hospital. The photographer told me, 'I wanted to make a dramatic picture. To be honest they don't tag toes. The tag was just lying on the body. I said, "Is it all right if I put it on his toe?" I felt awkward about it afterwards. In retrospect I don't think I should have done it, but I did.'

One of those who objected to this photograph, felt that it had been presented deliberately in a manner that would suggest it was one of the people in the Bedford Hospital. The features editor said that certainly was not the intention. He conceded that the tag should have been blurred, but the picture provided what he had asked for, a single strong image that worked with the text to encourage debate.

The whole story of this picture and our handling of it leaves the paper with a few things to think about. It has a policy of not interfering with images. This one had been both arranged and then altered. The photographer was perfectly frank about it: but none of that was known at the Guardian at the time the picture was published.

The photographer who took the picture at Bedford Hospital has given me an equally frank account of the events surrounding that – except for the way in which he got into the hospital.

He said serious thought was given to the possibility of relatives recognising the one person in the picture who was partially uncovered. 'We all sat down together and said, "Would you recognise your relative?" and we made a decision that you wouldn't be able to. With hindsight that was wrong.'

Six different families claimed to recognise their relative. One of them, however, was the real daughter of the partially visible man. 'The real family came in yesterday and it was a harrowing experience for all of us,' the photographer says. 'I met people who, unfortunately, I had put through the mill. They were magnanimous and understanding. They were much more interested to know what had gone on at the hospital, much more than any grievance with the press.'

He told me categorically that the picture he had taken, the one published on the front of G2, showed the room exactly as he had found it. Nothing was touched.

I leave you with one more question. Now that the identity of one of the people in the picture is known, should it be used again without the permission of the family?

Legal opinions: the thin line between 'facts' and lawsuits
→ 17 February 2001

Some of the more horrendous things that have appeared in the Guardian's daily corrections and clarifications column need not have found their way there if the journalists involved had had more sensitive alarm systems. The column over the past three years is dotted with examples of sometimes libellous statements that relied on 'facts' that proved to be otherwise, and found their way into the paper without setting off alarm bells.

To try to cut down the number of occasions on which this happens the paper has now introduced a series of short courses in the law as it affects journalism. Initially these are mainly for trainees and for journalists who have arrived without any instruction in relevant law.

The editor points out that the traditional route to the Guardian, through a job on a regional newspaper with a training course incorporating law for journalists on the way, is now by no means the one always followed. It cannot be assumed that everyone joining the editorial staff of the Guardian will have read Essential Law for Journalists, or Media Law, from cover to cover. The courses are an attempt to make good some of the deficiencies. Later they will be opened as 'master classes' to all editorial staff who feel they need to be reminded of or brought up to date on some aspects.

They are conducted by one of the Guardian's writers on the law, who is both a journalist and a lawyer. I went to the first one last week, on defamation. Basic points were emphasised: the possibility of libelling not just individuals, but companies, or even products. He made it clear that withholding the identity of a person who was the subject of a pejorative statement was no protection if the person could identify himself or herself, or be identified by others. Indeed if the person was a member of a small group it could lead to a defamation action from any one or all of them.

This session ended with a discussion of the House of Lords' judgment in the unsuccessful libel case brought against the Times and others by the former prime minister of Ireland, Albert Reynolds. Its conclusions appear to give reporters some protection when writing about public figures. The full significance is yet to be discovered.

The next session for the Guardian's journalists will be about contempt of court and restrictions on reporting. A third will consider such things as the protection of sources, the right to privacy, and the copyright laws. To colleagues who will get the opportunity to attend in the future, I cannot recommend these sessions too highly.

The purpose is to try to ensure that all journalists are aware of the legal environment in which they operate and that they know when something should be drawn to the attention of the lawyer.

This is not the same as leaving it to the lawyer. A previous editor of the Guardian told me that while it was good and necessary to have easy access to legal advice, it was essential that this did not stop journalists thinking for themselves. It was absolutely wrong to think of the lawyers as a safety net. They functioned best when advising on matters to which the journalist had already given some thought. The lawyers advised but the decision on whether or not to publish always remained an editorial one.

The former editor was not the only one to emphasise that the bedrock was facts and that it was the journalist's job to see that they were right. The Guardian's head of legal affairs made the same point: 'It is not the lawyer's job to check the facts.'

The Guardian now has a very good three-tier legal system. It has a team of four barristers, specialising in libel, who take turns on the news desk from 5 to 8pm every day. These libel lawyers, or night lawyers, are incredibly hard-working. They have about 300 stories placed before them in the course of an evening so clearly not a great deal of time is allowed for sucking the quill.

For the past four years the Guardian has also had its own in-house legal department (the last national broadsheet to acquire one). Then there is an outside legal firm which can be consulted when necessary.

The in-house legal affairs department has three lawyers dealing with editorial matters. They are there to be consulted, indeed like to be consulted, as far ahead of the planned publication date as possible. They are more than slightly miffed if given five minutes to read something that has been weeks or months in preparation. It sometimes happens. About 100 accusations of libel reach them in the course of a year. All but a tiny residue are resolved or rejected.

I consult the lawyers, among other reasons, to check that in my adjudication on a serious complaint (and before printing an apology) they share my opinion that I have been fair to the journalist, who could sue me if that were not the case.

Calculated risk: the art of publishing without being damned

→ 24 February 2001

With all that can be said, justly, against journalists, there is one kind of journalist to whom civilisation owes a very great debt, namely the brave and honest reporter who unearths and makes public unpleasant facts, cases of injustice, cruelty, corruption, which the authorities would like to keep hidden, and which even the average reader would prefer not to be compelled to think about. – WH Auden: A Certain World, 1970

Here is a question: is it ethical for a newspaper which campaigns for the reform of the libel laws to seek to use those laws to its advantage? Isn't that what a newspaper is doing when it says to its legal advisers, 'Yes, but will they sue?' – and then takes a calculated risk that they will not, and goes ahead with publication?

An element in the calculation may be the huge costs involved in pressing accusations of libel through the courts. To what extent should the nature of the person or organisation be considered? Is the importance of the story worth the risk? Is it a matter of imperative public interest? Do we believe that what we want to say is true?

A few more questions: are the libel laws as they exist more a tool to be used by the rich or powerful to smother the legitimate activities of the intrepid reporter, described above by Auden, than a necessary way to protect the innocent? Or are they really, in their present, rigorous form, much stronger, for instance, than those in the United States, a necessary brake on an irresponsible press?

Calculating the cost of defending and possibly losing libel actions in the English courts can induce dizzy spells. A newspaper's sense of purpose and resolve is tested in these sums. It has to be sure it is right. Many may believe – some Guardian journalists do – that the paper carries insurance against libel. It does not. It used to but the premiums themselves became punitive. When the paper goes to court to fight a libel action it does so knowing that the cost of losing (and sometimes the cost of winning) could represent a severe financial blow.

We shall come back to the question with which I started in a minute, but an essential thing to know is that the decision to publish is the editor's alone, and never the lawyer's. Similarly, it is his decision whether to concede or fight in the face of accusations of libel. It was his decision to fight the libel actions unsuccessfully brought against the paper by the former Conservative MPs Neil Hamilton and Jonathan Aitken. To take decisions of that kind you need great confidence in the journalists involved.

Last week I described the way in which the paper is trying to ensure that everyone on the editorial staff has a basic knowledge of the law affecting journalism. The second of its sessions for newly arrived journalists took place this week, and there will soon be open masterclasses that all Guardian journalists will be able to attend.

The idea, as I explained, is to see that individual journalists have reasonably efficient alarm systems, that they know, at least, when to exercise caution, and when to seek the very good legal advice that is always at hand.

One of the paper's most experienced investigative journalists says that learning about the law, the laws of defamation, and those covering official secrecy and contempt in particular, is essential if the journalist is to fulfil one of his or her essential functions, which is to challenge these laws. 'When I started, journalism seemed to consist of finding out things that the lawyer then told you you couldn't put in the paper. I started from the premise that freedom of speech was a good thing and that the law was a series of obstacles to be negotiated, and that could be negotiated if you knew what you were doing.

'So basically I believe that the journalist should have a confrontational rather than a compliant relationship with the law. The law is one of the key battlegrounds on which we fight for freedom of speech. But the only way you can take on the law is by knowing the law.'

Another investigative reporter emphasised the need to ensure the highest possible quality of evidence before coming to the question whether or not to publish serious allegations against an individual or organisation: 'Short of an admission from the subject, the best is, of course, irrefutable documentary evidence.' He concluded his comments to me this way: 'This is not to advocate excessive caution, just eternal vigilance.'

The editor of the paper says that the first question is: can we successfully defend this? Could we defend it if we went to court? 'Occasionally you might think, "Will they sue?" but I don't think that is exploiting the libel laws.'

The lawyers point out that it is not their job to prevent publication but to help publish as much as possible. Getting the stuff into the paper is the general idea.

I kid you not: the left-handed gunman who wasn't
→ 03 March 2001

Not long ago, when our Washington correspondent filed a report of moves in the United States to secure a posthumous pardon for Billy the Kid, we illustrated the story with a photograph of the famous outlaw. This is a ferrotype, or tintype, probably taken in 1880, the year he was captured by Sheriff Pat Garrett.

The photograph, familiar to all students of the West, but less so to the rest of us, shows Billy the Kid, full-length, the butt of his Winchester resting on the ground and the tip of the barrel gripped lightly in his right hand. More to the point, he carries his single-action Colt on his left hip, the handle pointing backwards.

To everyone involved in editing the page on which it appeared, everything seemed as it should be. Wasn't Billy, after all, a notorious left-hander – played as such by Paul Newman in Arthur Penn's 1958 film The Left-Handed Gun?

Almost immediately after the Guardian report appeared, I received an email from a reader: 'Your reproduction of the famous photograph of Billy the Kid is reversed. You can see by the waistcoat buttons and the belt buckle. This is a common error which has continued to reinforce the myth that Billy the Kid was left-handed. He was not. He was right-handed and carried his gun on his right hip.' The writer of the email was, it transpired, a former curator of the National Film and Television Archive of the British Film Institute, Clyde Jeavons.

His points about the buckle and buttons were indeed borne on closer examination. The prong on the belt buckle is pointing the wrong way, and the buttons run down the wrong side of his waistcoat. There is no doubt that what we are looking at is a reverse image.

Was it simply another case of 'flipping the picture'? After all, we have in the past presented readers of the Guardian with a photograph of an entirely left-handed orchestra and a flipped image of the Horsehead nebula. This case, however, did not prove so simple.

My correspondent produced further argument. 'This particular reproduction error has occurred so often in books and other publications over the years that it has led to the myth that Billy the Kid was left-handed, for which there is no evidence. On the contrary, the evidence (from viewing his photo correctly) is that he was right-handed: he wears his pistol on his right hip with the butt pointing backwards in a conventional right-handed draw position.'

He cites the Pictorial History of the Wild West by James D Horan and Paul Sann, 1954, in which the authors caption the 'correctly printed' picture: 'Billy the Kid. He was right-handed and carried his pistol on his right hip.'

Edward Buscombe, in The BFI Companion to the Western, 1988, now sadly out of print, while not commenting directly on the left hand/right hand issue, says this: 'There has probably been more tedious argument about the facts of Billy the Kid's life than about anything else in the West.' Alongside he prints the photograph to show the gun on Billy's right hip (buttons and buckle all in order) – the reverse of the Guardian's presentation.

A quick internet search produces vast quantities of information, including sites devoted to Billy the Kid which reproduce the image in question, usually showing it, as it appeared in the Guardian, with the pistol on the right of the picture – that is, on his left hip, if you regard it as you would a modern photograph.

The answer, in fact, is in the technique used to obtain the image in the first place. The tintype or ferrotype, to quote Britannica.com, was 'a positive photograph produced by means of a nitrocellulose (collodion) solution applied to a thin enamelled black iron plate immediately prior to exposure'. It says they remained a kind of folk art for the rest of the 19th century.

The best description I have found is in the online work, A History of Photography, compiled by Robert Leggat (www.rleggat.com/photohistory/). He makes the following essential point: 'The print would come out laterally reversed (as one sees oneself in a mirror) either people did not worry about this, or just possibly they did not discover it until after the photographer had disappeared!'

So the 'authentic' tintype of Billy the Kid, if one is to be purist about this, should be shown as it appeared in the Guardian, but pointing out that the image is reversed. If we want to see Billy the Kid the right way round, we have to grit our teeth, break our own rule forbidding the flipping of pictures, and reverse it again.

If you are still with me, the essential point in all this is that Billy the Kid was not, on the evidence of this image, left-handed. I find myself on the side of the right.

The Guardian carried the picture of Billy the Kid on February 3. Special thanks to Clyde Jeavons, who provided me with a good deal of the material for this column and to Edward Buscombe. A key book is Billy the Kid: A Short and Violent Life by Robert M Utley, University of Nebraska Press, 1989.

Out on a limb: a pose too frequently adopted
→ 10 March 2001

A reader looks askance at the Guardian's use of akimbo. He noticed a reference on the obituaries page to the 'arms akimbo' style of a footballer whose career was being remembered. 'I shall gently but pedantically point out,' he said, 'that akimbo has a very specific meaning: "with hand on hip and elbow bent outward" (my Chambers suggests that it comes from Middle English "in kenebowe"). [And probably, according to the Concise Oxford, from Old Norse before that.] To stand with arms akimbo is to assume the position of righteous indignation or amused tolerance or anger.'

What the writer of the obituary clearly meant, my correspondent said, was that the footballer ran around with spread or flapping arms and not with his hands constantly on his hips. The obituarist actually wrote this: 'His arms-akimbo style led his fellow England players to nickname him Flipper.'

We usually get this right. Here is an example from the work of Neville Cardus, remembering a speech by George Bernard Shaw in Manchester in May 1906 (quoted in an article in the Guardian by Shaw's biographer, Michael Holroyd): 'As he stood on the platform, arms akimbo, in tweeds and still the red flame of socialism in his beard, he told us to burn down Manchester town hall and the cathedral.' We get the picture.

We can visualise the golfing coach David Leadbetter correctly too in this description of him: 'the Englishman, who spends his days on the world's practice ranges, arms akimbo and long legs apart in a huge inverted V, is famous for his objectivity.' More about legs in a moment, but before that one final example of 'arms akimbo', this time from the women's pages, that provides an almost perfect illustration of the expression: 'Think pantomime dame with arms akimbo and ballooning crinoline.'

The Oxford English Dictionary, still hyphenating the word as 'a-kimbo' in the rather whiskery edition I have in front of me, provides just one unequivocal definition: 'Of the arms: In a position in which the hands rest on the hips and the elbows are turned outwards.'

The historical examples provided by the dictionary show the progress of the word towards us down the centuries, gradually assuming its recognisable present form, beginning with this quotation from about 1400: 'The hoost set his hond in kenebowe.'

It quotes Sir Thomas Urquhart from the mid-17th century: 'With gingling spurrs, and his arms a kenbol'; Sir Richard Steele, from the

Spectator of the early 18th century: 'She would clap her arms a kimbow'; Samuel Richardson in Clarissa (1748): 'She set her huge arms akembo'; and finally Robert Browning in 1879: 'Both arms a-kimbo.'

Nowhere, you will notice, is there any mention of legs. To return to my correspondent for a moment: ' "Legs akimbo" is something that I see in your paper even more frequently [than arms akimbo]. I think this is actually very witty if you know what the word means, but I'm increasingly of the opinion that no one does. Shame.'

Let us have a look. Here is something that appeared in a television programme note in one of our Saturday supplements, the Guide, recently: 'The acting then takes on Eldorado proportions and [the actor] stands defiantly, legs akimbo in a proverbial force 10, pissing into it.' One fears the worst.

Some of the paper's finest have fallen into the trap of mistakenly believing that akimbo simply means apart. Thus a photographer finds himself 'straining over my camera with tripod legs akimbo'. Many are caught 'legs akimbo on the sofa', among them Anne Robinson, discovered 'on her sofa in her black leather pants and her black boots and her black sleeveless T-shirt, knees up, legs akimbo'; and Liz Hurley, 'posing in a silver lame bikini with legs akimbo and tongue flickering provocatively'.

We have used it in the context of childbirth: 'Pregnant women are faced with two stark and equally unpalatable extremes: either submit legs akimbo to the stirrups…'.

You could perhaps present an argument that some of these examples were describing legs that had assumed roughly the same shape as arms when akimbo. It does not sound very convincing, does it?

The most interesting thing for me is the way in which this illustrates how easily we adopt into our vocabulary a word without referring to the dictionary to check its meaning. I could provide umpteen examples from the Guardian, but then so could you. But, for instance: the confusion of 'appraise' and 'apprise' has been annoying some of us – the first means to estimate the value or quality of something and the other means to inform, so you might certainly appraise your mum, as one columnist did recently, but you would not be apprising her of anything.

I am digressing. My advice is to keep your arms akimbo or you won't have a leg to stand on.

Cue jumping: the hunt for the real Fast Eddie – if there was one

→ 17 March 2001

Early last month we carried an obituary of an American pool player who called himself 'Fast Eddie' Parker, describing him, with no beating about the bush, as 'the man who inspired the film, The Hustler'. Just to remind you, The Hustler, released in 1961, was directed by Robert Rossen, and starred Paul Newman as the hustler of the title, Fast Eddie Felson.

A hustler in pool parlance is a gambling player prepared to lose a few games to increase the odds before he and his backers make their killing. We explained that while Fast Eddie Parker claimed to be the model for Fast Eddie Felson, he was not a hustler but a straight player who played his best in all circumstances.

We left no doubt, however, that he regarded himself as the main, or even the only, real contributor to the character of Fast Eddie Felson. A heading on his obituary read: 'Professional pool player who was the inspiration for Paul Newman's role in The Hustler.'

We said he had met Walter Tevis, the writer of the novel, The Hustler (1959), when the latter 'was working his way through college' and that 'Tevis borrowed one of Parker's aliases to create Fast Eddie Felson' – he claimed on other occasions that he had inspired Tevis to create first the character and hence the novel that was then adapted for the film.

Finally, we said that Parker had produced instructional books and videos that Paul Newman had used when preparing to revive the character of Fast Eddie Felson in Martin Scorsese's The Color of Money, 1986 (the screenplay written by Richard Price after the novel, The Color of Money, 1984, by Walter Tevis).

A few days after this obituary appeared I had a call from Eleanora Tevis, the widow of Walter Tevis (he died of lung cancer in August 1984), the first of a number of exchanges by phone and fax, essentially making the same point: 'Since The Hustler's publication in 1959 and the film's release in 1961, many pool players have claimed to be Fast Eddie Felson. Walter consistently stated that The Hustler was a work of fiction and the characters therein were fictitious.'

The exasperation Tevis felt is very well expressed in an article by Roy McHugh that appeared in a newspaper in Pittsburgh in 1983. McHugh said that people kept asking Tevis, in relation to another character in The Hustler, 'When did you first meet Minnesota Fats?' McHugh said Tevis cringed and wondered whether they would have asked Walt Disney, 'When did you meet Donald Duck?' (The person referred to here was Rudolf Walter Wanderone Jr. He had been playing under the name of New York Fats, in tribute to his birthplace, but changed his name to Minnesota Fats after Jackie Gleason created the part in The Hustler – see Britannica.com.)

This article was headed: 'All "Fast Eddies" say they're Hustler.' The piece was prompted by the death of a pool player called Edward 'Fast Eddie' Pelkey, and the agency wire at the time began: 'Edward "Fast Eddie" Pelkey, the famed pool shark portrayed by Paul Newman in the movie The Hustler, has died . . .' Tevis told Roy McHugh: 'I'm weary of explaining this. Nobody believes you when you keep telling them you invent your own characters.'

In 1987, after Eddie Parker had returned to live in his home territory of the Missouri Ozarks, he was interviewed by Bill Maurer from the local newspaper, the News-Leader. His report contains this sentence: 'Parker said he's been reluctant to acknowledge his role [the role he claimed as the model for Tevis's Fast Eddie] until recent years.'

Even more to the point, Maurer contacted four important people: the editor of a leading billiards magazine, the vice-president of the Professional Billiards Association, a professional pool player who had been active in the area where Parker said he met Tevis, and finally Tevis's boyhood friend who taught him to shoot pool. Maurer wrote: 'All four said they've never heard of Parker and questioned his role, if any, in influencing Tevis.'

To return to the instructional manuals and videos by Parker that Paul Newman is supposed to have used when preparing for The Color of Money. Mrs Tevis corresponded with Newman. She says he told her: 'Regardless of anything you've seen in the press, I didn't use any instructional books or tapes. Willie Mosconi taught me everything I knew and was my instructor during the entire film, as well as the technical director.' Willie Mosconi (see Britannica.com again), an American pocket billiards player, was world champion 15 times between 1941 and 1957. He died in 1993.

We carried the obituary because of the connection with the character of Fast Eddie Felson, a connection, wouldn't you agree, that the most generous person would describe as extremely tenuous?

*The Hustler is published in Britain by Bloomsbury
(which also publishes Tevis's novel, The Man
Who Fell to Earth, filmed with David Bowie).*

Lobby fodder: the use of mass email campaigns
→ 31 March 2001

With the electronic media has come the electronic lobby. We are still not quite sure how to respond to it. We have encountered it now in a number of causes: the Guardian's alleged unfairness to the Blair government in the early months after the election (I dispute that there was a significant lobby at work there but some of my colleagues disagree) the alleged demonisation of the Serbian people in our coverage of the war over Kosovo and most recently and most vigorously the paper's alleged anti-Israeli prejudice. The pro-Arab or pro-Palestinian lobby, which exists, is not on anything like such a large scale.

The pro-Israel lobby – that is what it is in intent if not always in effect – can mean two or three hundred organised emails piling into a queue in the paper in the space of a few hours and threatening to clog up the works.

Lobby emails, on any issue, are usually easy to recognise. Very often they simply follow a pattern provided by the organiser, but variations usually retain headings or phrases from the original which clearly indicate their source. Some newspapers after sampling a couple erase the rest unread.

The New York Times, which I visited recently, has been coping with one lobby accusing the paper of minimising 'the protests surrounding the presidential inauguration'. The paper's recorded message on its reader comment line, says: 'If you're calling as an individual about a correction, or with a coverage question we can answer – and not as part of a group campaign – we will try to reply.'

The comment editor of the Guardian wrote about the pro-Israel lobby on his pages a few weeks ago tracing one significant part of it to an organisation based in London. His section is a favourite target. The letters page of the Guardian is another. In both cases, you might fairly say, well, they would be. Individual journalists who write about the Middle East in the Guardian are also bombarded with emails, some abusive in the extreme. The most abusive are reserved for colleagues who are Jewish.

The comment editor is now reluctant to provide email addresses at the end of pieces which might provoke what he calls hate mail. He feels that the experience of the past weeks has strengthened the case for a parallel email network to ensure that messaging around the office is not jeopardised by the mass invasion of personal queues.

The lesson of lobbies of this kind, on this scale, is that they are perceived by most of those on the receiving end, not as the bearers of reasonable argument but as bullying and inhibiting to real debate. The message is seen to be the threatening weight of numbers.

These lobbies have been described to me as potentially counter-productive by others seeking to promote Israeli views by different means. One said that the noise created by this stimulated clamour of voices crowding in all together was drowning out attempts at more reasonable discourse. An organisation which seeks to promote Arab views, and which uses what might be called selective email lobbying, says that if it saw signs that the mass-email lobby was succeeding, it would certainly change its own tactics to do the same.

Each side in the present conflict in the Middle East has accused the Guardian of favouring the other. Some journalists say, that is OK then, we must be getting it right if both sides are complaining. The other possibility, as another colleague pointed out, was that we were getting it wrong in both directions.

One of the problems for the paper is that lobbies, large or small, almost always include a great many people who do not normally read the Guardian, whose attention has been drawn to a particular report or article in the paper and who therefore see it removed from the context of the Guardian's coverage as a whole. They are unaware, perhaps, of one important fact, that the comment pages always, but especially with reference to conflicts (the Gulf war, the wars in former Yugoslavia for example), seek to provide a platform for the widest range of opinion. They do that independently of the Guardian's leader line.

The editor had this in mind when he formulated a model email of his own, to be used at the discretion of Guardian journalists, to reply to senders of emails criticising the paper's Israel coverage. In it he rejects any accusation that the coverage 'indicates a strong bias against Israel'. He lists commentators from all sides of the conflict, and concludes: 'I believe the paper has distinguished itself in the depth, range and breadth of its reporting and commentary.'

Whether we like it or not, the email lobby is here to stay. It is a natural product of a democratic medium. If I thought it worth saying in a situation which generates such high passion, I would add, 'But please, let's be reasonable.'

Sacred rights: the pitfalls of direct translation
→ 07 April 2001

In a recent report about a dispute between two Italian novelists, Ippolita Avalli and Susanna Tamaro, we said the narrator in a book by Ms Avalli had thrown a tantrum during mass and called the congregation 'whitewashed tombs'. A reader was immediately in touch to say: surely this is a mistranslation and should have been 'whited sepulchres'? It probably should have been, because although our correspondent's translation was literally correct it deprived the expression of any real force as invective. Didn't it?

I suspect that behind the complaint was the suspicion that our correspondent had not recognised the source of the expression. There is a recurring background lament that no one at the godless Guardian knows the Bible, a reflection of the argument that our increasing inability to read the Biblical or classical allusions in paintings, for example, renders the contents of the National Gallery in London virtually meaningless.

What Ms Avalli's protagonist actually called the people in church was *'sepolcri imbiancati'*, a quotation from, to be specific, Matthew 23:27. The nearest office copy of an English-Italian dictionary (dated 1990) has the following entry: *Un sepolcro imbiancato* – a whited sepulchre, a hypocrite.

In the noble and, in this case, self-explanatory English of the King James version, this is: 'Woe unto you, scribes and Pharisees, hypocrites! for ye are like unto whited sepulchres, which indeed appear beautiful outward, but are within full of dead men's bones, and of all uncleanness.'

The New English Bible, honourably in pursuit of more accessible meaning at some expense to the poetry, says, 'You are like tombs covered with whitewash.' The New Oxford Annotated Bible (1994) offers this version: 'Woe to you, scribes and Pharisees, hypocrites! For you are like whitewashed tombs [our correspondent's very phrase], which on the outside look beautiful, but inside they are full of the bones of the dead and of all kinds of filth.'

There is a useful footnote: tombs were whitewashed before Passover so that Jewish travellers might not unwittingly touch them and become ceremonially unclean.

As usual we are watching words in motion, in this case the receding of a phrase quoted to lend a grand Biblical authority to an accusation of hypocrisy. Brewer's Dictionary of Phrase and Fable says: 'A whited sepulchre: a hypocrite, especially one who conceals wickedness under a cloak of virtue, etc.' We shall wait a little while, I think, before it is replaced by an entry for 'whitewashed tomb'. It falls rather limply on the air.

However, it escaped the Guardian's daily corrections column. So did the following because, even though it resulted from a slip of the finger on the keyboard, and though the author, an expert on aspects of the countryside, could be heard clapping a hand to his forehead when it was pointed out to him, it was not absolutely wrong.

This is what he said, in the context of a piece exploring the possibility that foot and mouth disease may provide an opportunity to change the approach to sheep farming: 'The old "weathers" can lead the flock to safety when the snow clouds gather.'

This brought a complaint from a reader who said 'weathers' should be wethers and that there was no need to enclose it in quotes because it was a perfectly legitimate word. Mistakes of this kind are often seen by readers, especially those who live in the lands beyond the M25, as symptoms of our separation from the countryside. We have to exonerate this particular contributor, who reaches Farringdon Road with a convincing amount of mud on his boots.

The reader who complained is right, of course, although it seems rather picky to find fault in such a beautifully descriptive sentence – beautifully descriptive, that is, if you know what a wether is.

The Oxford English Dictionary is, as usual, very entertaining on the subject. Its first definition is 'a male sheep, a ram especially a castrated ram. See also Bell-wether' (which we shall in a moment). It gives examples of this use from the ninth to the 19th centuries, with the spelling wether shedding all variants by the present time, including the most common one, which was 'weather'. The latter was the version that Shakespeare used in his poem The Passionate Pilgrim: 'My weathers bell rings dolefull knell' and as a metaphor for a eunuch, in the Merchant of Venice: 'I am a tainted Weather of the flocke, Meetest for death.'

And so to bellwether. The OED offers three definitions: the leading sheep of a flock, on whose neck a bell is hung; a chief or leader (contemptuous); and a clamorous person, one ready to give mouth.

A final quotation (also courtesy the OED) from the philosopher GH Lewes (1847): 'Men are for the most part like sheep, who always follow the bell-wether.' On that note I shall ring off.

Border lines: words that leave a bad taste in the mouth
→ 21 April 2001

Bad taste and good taste are easily defined. I have good taste and you have bad taste. The formula is the same for each of us. The question is: what place does bad taste have in a newspaper? The most frequent causes of complaint are the cartoons and diaries, particularly the cartoons of Steve Bell and the Diary by Matthew Norman which usually appear side by side on the Comment and Analysis page – at the heart of the paper, you might say.

It is usually readers, rather than those depicted, who are deeply offended by cartoons, whereas it is often, but not always, the subjects of diary items who complain. In most of these complaints, bad taste is the accusation. Those upset by cartoons write to the editor, they write to me, occasionally they write to the Press Complaints Commission and sometimes to their MP. All these complaints are taken seriously and considered by me and by those involved.

Every time the diary refers to the alopecia of the editor of the Sun I get a call or two from people who say, go ahead, attack the editor of the Sun, but alopecia is not funny. One retaliated with the demand that the Guardian publish a photograph of the diarist so that 'we alopecian/slappy baldies (possibly including the editor of the Sun) can gawp in envy and reverence at his luxuriantly fecund follicles, of which he is so proud'. The diarist has given his own response to that this week.

But you see how personal it gets? Where do you draw the line? When the diarist went further and suggested that the editor of the Sun should be sectioned, that is (Collins dictionary) 'confined in a mental hospital under an appropriate section of the mental health legislation', a reader who had been so confined until released by an appeal tribunal wrote to protest.

'It is an extremely frightening and disturbing experience. I don't wish to be humourless about the issue of mental health, but is this gag really so amusing, and so vital to the column, that it needs to be made so repeatedly and so thoughtlessly?' I am with the reader on this. The time to lay off from the diarist's point of view surely must be when he begins to evoke sympathy for the victim.

One reader a couple of years ago complained to both his MP and the PCC about a cartoon by Martin Rowson. He thought a reference to the Blairs represented an unacceptably vulgar attack on the whole Blair family, and the concept of the family in general, in terms that were 'in extremely bad taste to say the least'. The cartoonist, in this case, offered his own interpretation of the cartoon and a personal apology to the reader.

The complaint hinged on an interpretation of the words 'The Pope is Catholic, the Blairs shit in the woods'. The cartoonist said he was simply varying two common ways of expressing the obvious: 'Is the Pope a Catholic? Do bears shit in the woods?'

This exchange ended with a good-natured but grudging acceptance by the reader of what he called 'a quasi apology'. No one who complains about this kind of thing is, in my experience, ever satisfied by the explanation offered by cartoonist, diarist or columnist or, indeed, by anyone on the paper.

In replying to the MP who took up the complaint about the Rowson cartoon, I said: 'Guardian cartoonists are given as much freedom as possible and often tread a narrow path of acceptability. Their audience turns to them for this. This cartoon probably strayed over the boundary.'

I meant that. But where is the boundary? It is rarely easy to determine. Editing cartoons is quite difficult. Steve Bell's cartoons, for example, are not preceded by sketches for approval. The cartoonist working for the main comment pages enjoys the same status as the paper's top columnists. Alterations are made rarely and in haste. Sometimes a cartoon misfires.

One recent example was an attempt to combine a comment on the Selby train crash and the spread of foot and mouth disease. Two sheep are looking at the wreckage, one saying: 'I blame these intensive methods of transport', the other adding '. . . or maybe it's just a crap time of the year.'

It made a number of people angry because it came over as a flippant comment on a crash, this time not the fault of the railways, in which people had been killed. The cartoonist agrees it did not work and says he can understand the complaints because he never satisfactorily worked out his own intentions. Should we have withheld it from publication? Perhaps.

How would we have handled artists such as Gillray or Rowlandson or any of the great satirical writers of two centuries ago? As our diarist said, 'No one objects to their kind of cruelty with hindsight.'

So long as they are scrutinising the performance of our politicians and public figures, and mocking their pretensions, do we mind if they step over the boundary of 'taste' now and then?

Inside story: a letter to a fellow Guardian columnist
→ 19 May 2001

Dear Erwin, I enjoyed meeting you and talking to you in prison the other day. Forgive me for using your pen name rather than your real name but since I have chosen to write to you in the slightly awkward form of an open letter, I thought it better to address you by the name you have used to sign the fortnightly column – A Life Inside – which has been appearing in the Guardian (in the tabloid second section, G2), for more than a year now.

In that time you have won many fans both outside prison and inside. I was amused to hear that some of your fellow prisoners have adopted the nicknames you have given them in your column. And I know one of the letters you have had was from a lawyer who said he had been waiting for 50 years for someone to write about prisons in the way that you do.

I can understand that reaction. Over the years I have read a great deal about prison, both fact and fiction, but nothing quite so straightforward and direct and often very moving as the scenes from prison life that you give us, and certainly nothing like it in a newspaper.

Apart from the fact that you write enviably well you do it with an easy and unaffected humanity. I don't think we have to know much about prison life to see this as something quite remarkable, reflecting credit on you but also on many of those who have been responsible for you in various prisons. It speaks volumes about the long, long journey that you have made and, I know you would agree, which you couldn't have made if you had not confronted your crimes and the effect of what you did on others, if you hadn't, so to speak, faced yourself as you were.

As you know, when we carried the first of your regular 'dispatches on prison life', in February last year, we prefaced it with the note 'Erwin James has to date served 16 years of a life sentence for two murders.' And we have always added a line pointing out that you do not get paid for your contributions. The form this takes now is a note at the end saying 'Erwin James is serving a life sentence. The fee for this article will be paid to charity.' In fact the money goes to the Prisoners' Advice Service, which you nominated and which has helped you in the past.

When readers have questioned me about these arrangements I have written privately to them, saying, among other things, that they seem to me to have been made in an exemplary fashion, with the full cooperation of the Home Office and with a lot of care and thought by the features editor of the Guardian and his colleagues.

One or two readers have seemed inclined to believe that the

arrangement for, let's call it, non-payment is one imposed by the Guardian to exploit your situation to the paper's advantage – journalists are not exactly near the summit of public esteem. In fact, earlier this week I spoke to the writer who introduced you to the Guardian and he said that he had advised you not to accept payment and you had agreed – before either of you knew that the rules, in any case, forbade it.

So far as we are concerned there are two sets of rules to be considered. The first are the prison rules which contain a straightforward ban on the transmission by convicted prisoners of material intended for publication in return for payment. The others are the self-imposed rules set out in the code of the Press Complaints Commission which all newspapers say they will abide by. The relevant bit of this bars payment to convicted criminals 'except where the material ought to be published in the public interest and payment is necessary for this to be done'.

I don't believe that this applies, or was ever intended to apply, to the kind of thing you have been writing for the Guardian or for anything similar that you might write after your eventual release. Suppose, for example, that you wrote a column called A Life Outside about the trials, if that's not too evocative a word, of adjustment. In my mind there is no reason why an ex-prisoner should not be paid for that kind of thing. You do not write about your crimes. You certainly do not glamorise crime in general.

It sounds patronising to talk about the rehabilitative value for you of your writing. You told me how good for you it has been writing the column. But perhaps we should talk about the value of what you are doing for the rest of us.

I know that a former governor of a prison where you spent some years has said you are the only prisoner he has kept in touch with in his retirement. Your probation officer, just about to retire, told me that he will give you his home address and an invitation to keep in touch with him when you meet for the last time in prison.

I look forward to reading you in future, so don't stop writing. Best wishes, Ian Mayes.

Nobody's perfect: how even Guardian legends could get it wrong

→ 02 June 2001

Universal errors are correct – Arabic proverb

Some of you, when you write to me to complain of a factual inaccuracy or grammatical lapse, add a note lamenting a general decline in standards perceived in many years of reading the paper, beginning in its days as the Manchester Guardian. Occasionally you demand that the offender be taken out and shot.

It is clearly true, to me anyway, that there are more mistakes of one kind or another in the paper of today than in the paper of 20, 30, 50 years ago. The vast acres of the modern paper provide a much greater opportunity for them, and as you may see for yourselves in the daily corrections and clarifications column, we have not hesitated to seize it.

To point out that the golden age of unblemished prose and unimpeachable fact is mythical is not to be cruel or complacent. It is to be accurate. Some of you, triumphantly and accusatorially, invoke the memory of CP Scott, the great editor of the Manchester Guardian whose stern, bewhiskered face gazes over the morning meetings of the present editor. Your point is that the things of which you complain would not have happened in Scott's day.

They did, alas, and Scott was involved in the same frustrating struggle, on a scale in his case that held out a tantalisingly closer prospect of success. WP Crozier, who was editor from 1932 to 1944, in a chapter he contributed to a biography – CP Scott of the Manchester Guardian by JL Hammond, 1934 – described Scott's way with error and correction.

'He desired to bring the niceties of correct usage to the general notice, but not to do anything which might pillory an individual. "Could one suggest," he asked, "any easy method by which correction of the little errors could be made generally available without offence?"' So, no taking out and shooting. Crozier, a little wearily perhaps, noted that a method was suggested to Scott and accepted by him in principle but never applied in practice. The path of error is littered with unapplied principles.

Crozier says Scott's preferred method of censure was 'to send little notes, pinning the cutting at the top of a scrap of paper'. Today we wash our dirty linen in public, but in the great majority of cases still allow the journalist the saving grace of anonymity.

But how did CP Scott himself respond to correction. Not, apparently, with great enthusiasm. Crozier writes: 'Unless plain error was discovered, it was well to resist suggestions that "CP's" words should be improved. It is known that Homer nodded, but not what Homer said when he was told about it.' However, he adds, 'For reasonable corrections ["reasonable", presumably, by his own definition] "CP" sent down a note of thanks. "I'm glad you did," he would say, "very stupid of me!"'

Scott was particularly attentive to the paper's use of English. 'The man who passed "seaward journey to the great metropolis," and when the copy came back to him, found written in firm blue pencil "voyage to London" knew what sort of English "CP" liked.'

Scott disapproved of foreign words ('Why do they say "portfolio" when they mean an English "ministry"?') Americanisms ("showdown" for example) puns ("Tragedy in reel life") and any laxity in usage. "Look at this," he said, "Blank died literally in harness". He didn't.'

A colleague of Scott's, William Haslam Mills, observed in an essay to mark the centenary of the Manchester Guardian in 1921 '[Scott] is the only member of his own staff who understands clearly when the conjunction should be "nor" and when it should be "or", and when one follows the other, what happens next.' Crozier says a running debate about the placement and purpose of the comma was ended only by the onset of the summer holidays.

This all sounds very familiar. Neville Cardus (in Conversations with Cardus by Robin Daniels, 1976) recalled how Scott had told him off for allowing Ernest Newman, the music critic, whom Cardus revered, to use the phrase, 'The concert commenced . . .' rather than 'began'.

Long after Scott had departed Cardus recalled how in the 60s he telephoned a review from Edinburgh which included the sentence, 'In spite of the difficulty of this music, she was quite eloquent.' This came out the next day as, 'She was a white elephant.' A clean sheet is simply a dream.

To conclude with a Spanish proverb: He is always right who suspects that he is always making mistakes.

Sincerely yours: the value, and the hazards, of the letters page

→ 23 June 2001

Editing letters to the editor for publication is probably one of the most difficult jobs on the Guardian. The clamour for publication is understandable. Those who make it to the platform have the opportunity to address well over one million people.

Since I last wrote about letters (January 31 1998), the potential audience has grown enormously with the development of the Guardian Unlimited network. All the letters that appear in the paper are on the website, one click from the home page (www.guardian.co.uk).

There is clearly room for further development here. In normal times about 300 letters a day are directed at the newspaper letters page and about 20 are printed, some of them quite brief. At the moment fewer letters are arriving, perhaps due to post-election torpor. The point is that all the letters to the Guardian intended for publication could in theory be posted on the website.

Nothing would more quickly earn the letters editor the grudging respect of the most frustrated letter writer than this. I say in theory, though, because in practice some would have to be withheld for legal reasons, some because they would expose a degree of idiosyncrasy rather greater than that to which readers of the page are accustomed.

But it would be an interesting exercise to try, if only once: to put up as many of one day's letters as possible and invite you, the readers, to select and edit about 20 of them, giving prominence to the important topic of the day, retaining the salient points in the letters selected. You would then be able to compare your selection with the one actually published.

By the way, the editor of the Guardian, and the lawyer, see the selected letters before publication every day. You, though, would be looking at an array of 200 to 300 already 'legalled'.

The letters editor, the mediator and custodian of the platform, has to be constantly vigilant for those who would use it for questionable purposes. At the same time, she has to allow the freest possible range of opinion and produce a lively and entertaining read.* Complaints about selection, usually seen by those not selected as exclusion or rejection, and complaints about editing are not altogether rare.

Very rarely, however, a letter gets through should not have been published at all. A recent example was one carried at the time of the riots in Oldham suggesting that young Muslims had been encouraged to attack Hindu homes and shops. I was alerted to this by a Muslim reader who felt that the letter, which appeared to be from a Muslim, in fact was not.

When I tried to contact the writer of the letter – which had arrived, as the great majority now do, by email – I found that the postal address he had given was false. I then emailed him inviting him to call me. On the telephone the following day he explained that, yes, the address was false – he had to be careful because he was a Christian Pakistani involved in anti-Muslim propaganda (I shall allow myself an exclamation mark)! Our own reporter found no evidence of the phenomenon described in the letter. A note appeared in the corrections column saying that publication of the letter was regretted.

I use it as an example of two things: the need for extra vigilance in particularly volatile situations, and the strength of attraction of the letters page as a platform.

There is little that is too controversial to be carried these days. In passing, I had a conversation this week with Mary Crozier, who edited the letters from about 1946 to 1956, through the editorship of AP Wadsworth into the early months of Alastair Hetherington's tenure. Crozier and Wadsworth had preserved the custom, originating in CP Scott's time, of not publishing letters of religious controversy. 'They were always so ill-natured,' she said. Hetherington lifted the ban.

The letters page is among the more important parts of the paper. It has remained the paper's principal forum of reader opinion despite the increase in direct email correspondence with journalists, and the growth in popularity of the letters pages in the Weekend magazine and in some of the specialist sections: Online, Education, and Society, which made room for letters on its redesign. Media, oddly perhaps, has yet to open this particular line of communication.

Letters for publication should not be sent to me. The front door is: letters@guardian.co.uk

* The letters editor has changed since this was written and is now Nigel Willmott.

Mind your language: the need for sensitivity in matters of mental health

→ 14 July 2001

A former editor of the Guardian, AP Wadsworth, once wrote: 'All journalists like to think that sometimes they influence other people; that is their endearing frailty.' I like to think that, because it was in the Guardian that he was writing, he might have said 'their enduring frailty'. I did believe, and I continue to believe (wilfully perhaps) that journalists can help to change things for the better, and certainly in the area of prejudice.

If you say that the media offer an unrivalled opportunity to combat rather than reinforce prejudice, it is likely to provoke laughter, or perhaps tears. But the signals that newspapers send out, or that they reflect back to us, play a significant part in telling us who we are and in what kind of world we live.

The great Austrian satirist of the late 19th and early 20th centuries, Karl Kraus, had an interesting comment: 'The world has become uglier since it began to look in a mirror every day so let us settle for the mirror image and do without an inspection of the original. It is uplifting to lose one's faith in a reality which looks the way it is described in a newspaper.'

The pessimistic or heavily ironic view of newspapers that Karl Kraus proposed is easily sustained today if that is your inclination. Look, for instance, at the way in which media-fanned hysteria about paedophiles led to an attack on a paediatrician, a shaming example for all of us of the effects of prejudice, ignorance and irresponsibility.

Nevertheless I persist in believing that journalism can have a positive effect on prejudices that make life more difficult for people for whom it is difficult enough already. Prejudice produces stigma, and it seems to me obvious that the prejudices associated with mental illness often add to the misery of the person who is ill, and tend to slow recovery or at least impede tolerance and understanding.

It seems astonishing that in the 21st century we still need to talk about it. Stigma is an effect of society lying about itself. We know, but seem to want to deny, that huge numbers of us will experience mental illness at some time during our lives. Few of us will go through our lives without some close experience, through a relative or friend or colleague, of mental illness. And those of us who have had that close experience may have seen something of the courage and dignity of those with these conditions – attributes not often acknowledged in the media in this context.

Criminality involving the mentally ill seems to be of much more interest, with the consequence that there is a wildly exaggerated view of the number of those likely to be a danger to others (a tiny number, much smaller than those who are likely to harm themselves).

The least a newspaper can do is to accept that the language it uses in reference to mental illness is important and to demonstrate this recognition in practice. There are problems. Journalists hate the slightest restriction: they may cry 'political correctness' and need considerable persuasion that what is being suggested is simply consideration for others. Some do not get the point at all and will insist on flouting the paper's policy, clearly set out in the style guidelines, which may be seen on our website.

This week, once again, a reader sent in a cutting with a ring round a passage where the word schizophrenic had been misused: 'You have to be slightly schizophrenic if you date someone outside your scene.' About a year ago we used the word to describe the decor of a new restaurant: 'It's completely schizophrenic inside, owing a little to its being cobbled from two buildings.'

The term, when used loosely or flippantly and in non-medical contexts, is being quite deliberately pushed out of the Guardian, with readers ready to pounce on it every time it appears. When I wrote about this in October 1998 I found that in the previous year terms such as schizophrenia had been misused in the Guardian in the great majority of about 150 references. When I checked again this week, again going back one year, I found that the number of references was about the same (154) but less than a dozen constituted serious misuse. I suppose that is some kind of progress.

We are trying to move away from the superficiality satirised in an episode of Absolutely Fabulous, in which Dawn French, playing the part of a television hostess, said, 'And later we'll be taking an in-depth look at acute schizophrenia – that will be from 9.20 to 9.23.'

This is adapted from a short talk given to the
annual meeting of the Royal College of Psychiatrists.
Thanks to Nick Dastoor who did some research
for this column. Copies of a leaflet produced by
the National Union of Journalists, Shock Treatment,
a guide to better mental health reporting,
free from 020-7278 7916, email acorn.house@nuj.org.uk

Picfalls: how errors can arise in pictures and captions
→ 21 July 2001

In an average week about 1,500 photographic images are used throughout the printed editions of the Guardian. Like other broadsheets, the paper has become much more pictorial. An unillustrated or under-illustrated page may now in the changed environment assume a leaden aspect, rather like dead air in a broadcast. If an editor, looking at a plan or proof of a page says, 'a bit texty' it is criticism not praise.

Pictures are (or should be) an active, not passive element on a page. When things go right, as they do most of the time, pictures, text and headlines work together to convey the content accurately and vividly. They encourage us to read and understand. But such is the pressure to illustrate that desperation sometimes drives and picfalls – let us call them – are encountered.

Picfalls come in many forms. Here are some of the things we can do (and have done): we can use a picture of the wrong person; we can use a picture of the wrong place; we can flip or reverse pictures (most ambitiously, we reversed the Horsehead nebula); we can use the right picture but the wrong caption (sometimes because the picture has been changed between editions but the original caption has remained). These are minor picfalls.

Unfortunately there are major picfalls and the consequences of our failure to avoid them may be serious offence to individuals, or damage to their, or their company's, reputation. A column of a few months ago saying uncomplimentary things about estate agents (who appear to occupy the same stratum of public esteem as, say, journalists) was illustrated by a 'for sale' sign on which the name of an estate agent was clearly visible. The lawyer, alas, did not see the page with the two things together – the general remarks of the text, expressing opinions which the columnist had a perfect right to, and the identification of one specific agent who had nothing whatsoever to do with the story. It was a totally unwarranted slur by association and an appropriate apology was made.

This kind of picfall, stumbled into carelessly, should be easily avoided. Translate the situation so that it refers to you. Journalists are a disreputable bunch of incompetents who hardly ever get anything right, and here is a picture of Ian Mayes.

More recently a report tracing the experiences of an illegal immigrant mentioned a period of work with an exploitative fairground dodgem track. This was illustrated with a picture of a dodgem track totally unrelated to the accompanying story and to the events described in it. However, the dodgem track in our illustration was unique and therefore instantly recognisable to those who had seen it – and instantly recognisable to the owner. She also complained of slur by association. We published a full apology for this, too.

Attentive readers may sometimes come across tortuous captions that attempt to put some distance between the illustration and the sentiments expressed or the events described in the accompanying article. Try to think of a form of words that would have persuaded the estate agent that there was no harm at all in using a picture of one of his boards in the context mentioned above. Or that would have persuaded the owner of the dodgem track that she had been treated to some innocuous free publicity. These writhings almost always mean that the picture is inappropriate and that using it is, from the paper's point of view, asking for trouble.

The caption is occasionally the culprit. Are all the people in the photograph of a pitch invasion – accompanying a report about the risk of injury to players – 'fans', as the caption said? It turns out that they are not. One, clearly identifiable, is a steward who is running on to the pitch to try to protect the players. He is doing his job, in other words. Whether a journalist handling the picture might have guessed as much, is itself a matter for conjecture. The steward had a justifiable complaint and the paper apologised to him.

On another recent occasion we published a picture of a bank of cricket fans captioned 'racist taunts by England's Barmy Army'. There was nothing in the accompanying report to justify the association of the supporters who gather under this banner with racism, and neither is there anywhere else. Another apology.

Occasionally these captioning errors have a wide resonance. A picture of Palestinian children playing war games, in which we said Israeli soldiers shot Palestinians (following the picture agency's caption) proved on close scrutiny to be the other way round. It took a long time to check, but we did and we corrected it and so did the agency. But, just to keep things in perspective, read my first sentence again.

Blurred vision: pictures that confuse reality and fiction
→ 28 July 2001

This is going to be a column with more questions than answers. A few weeks ago we published in one of our Saturday supplements, the Guide, a picture, in colour, of a young woman impaled on a picket fence. She lay, face upwards with open eyes, her body pierced just below the breast by two blood-covered stakes of the fence, her skirt raised and her legs apart. One person complained about the picture: what should he say to his six-year-old son who, not long after the paper arrived that Saturday morning, had asked about it? He told him it was make-believe from a film – a still, in fact, from what the Guide itself described as a 'low-budget werewolf flick' called Ginger Snaps. Beyond that, he confessed, he was at a loss what to say.

I said he should tell his son it was a mistake to use it and to say we were sorry we did. Some of you may already be thinking, why the fuss? It was just a film. The boy's father – a photographer who had worked in war zones – wanted to know what distinction we made between fantasy and reality in judging whether a gruesome image should be used, and we shall come to that.

Here are a few other points. The boy would not have been allowed to see the film from which the still was taken. He would not have seen it in a trailer either. It is extremely unlikely that he would have seen anything like it on television even if he was unusually late to bed. To what extent should the paper worry about exposing children to images of this kind? Does the paper have any responsibilities here, or is it up to parents to protect their children if they feel it to be necessary? Does it really matter?

The boy's father again: 'Maybe it doesn't make any difference. When I was his age growing up in Alabama, the next-door neighbour girl brought out her county sheriff father's crime-scene photo album. I found it very disturbing and we were all told off later. I have grown up normal – relatively. I was a news photographer in central America in the 1980s, so I know what the real thing looks like and I have my albums too. I supported the Guardian on the war-dead pictures. That I am willing to explain to my son.'

The picture in the Guide he felt was 'gratuitous and demeaning for all of us'. 'How can I explain that this picture means nothing and the [news] pictures in the front section mean a lot?'

I have a friend who is a child psychiatrist and who worked among the war-traumatised children of Bosnia. He sympathised with a parent called upon to explain to a child the picture of the impaled young woman. He made the point that the more clearly an image was fictional the less disturbing it was likely to be (which explains, in part, why we usually find cartoon violence acceptable). He noted that the Guide was entirely devoted to entertainment and therefore provided a context which would clearly signal to everyone, except perhaps young children, that the image in question was fictional.

The fact remained, however, that this picture, with what the reader who complained called its 'entertainment gore', required a lot of explanation. Why did people find it entertaining or funny? Then there was the strong sexual element, with connotations of cruelty and voyeurism.

The psychiatrist believed that young children should be protected from images such as this. How would we achieve that? Simply by not using them? Would you call that censorship or editing?

But back to reality, so to speak. One thing we agreed upon, and that my correspondent agreed, too, was the need to carry pictures that brought home the truth about war. John Pilger, writing in the Guardian earlier this week, about the picture of the Iraqi soldier burnt to a cinder at the wheel of his vehicle on the Basra Road, said: 'That single image demolished the propaganda that war had at last become a bloodless science: "clean" and "surgical".'

The psychiatrist said, 'Some pictures are shown knowing that they are going to be shocking – and they should be shown because they are shocking. The truth is terribly important to people in war zones. They say people don't understand what is going on here on the ground.'

My correspondent again, 'There should be no illusions about the horror of war and the consequences of violence.'

I think there is a test: is it a war picture or an anti-war picture? Pictures in the Guardian, the publication of which I have defended in the past, and which came into the anti-war category in my mind, were the front page photograph of a young woman who hanged herself in Bosnia, and the front-page picture of a woman killed by bombing in Kosovo.

One last question among the many remaining – what about the children in these cases?

Knowing our place: location, location, location
→ 04 August 2001

A report in the Guardian last Tuesday, forecasting a rainy end to the heatwave that 'Britain' was having, included the following: 'By Saturday, temperatures will be back to 16C in the far north of Scotland and 20–21C in the north of Britain.' An email from a New Zealand reader arrived almost immediately: 'Call me a dumb Kiwi [certainly not], but . . . are these not the same thing?'

Indeed they are and this, perhaps, was no more than a little slip between friends – in this case, 'Britain' for 'England'. But frequently repeated, as this kind of error is, it has led some readers to conclude, quite understandably, that at any given moment we do not know where the hell we are, or, worse, that we know where 'we' are – which is usually in central London – and we do not give a damn where 'you' are.

Before we reach the end of this column we must see if we can come to an accommodation, but already I have the feeling that this is an unattainable goal. Almost all the terms we use to describe the parts, or combinations of parts, of the islands we inhabit are satisfactory only up to a point. England, Scotland and Wales sound simple and specific enough. But what precisely do we mean when we say English? Is it not the same as British? Are, for instance, England football supporters 'English' until trouble breaks out, when, from a certain viewpoint, they conveniently become 'British'? We are already waist-deep and sinking.

We have still to come to Britain, Great Britain, Northern Ireland, Ulster, Ireland, the United Kingdom, the British Isles . . . Here are relevant definitions from the Guardian style guide.

Britain/UK : These terms are synonymous, despite what you might have been told. Britain is the official short form of United Kingdom of Great Britain and Northern Ireland. Used as adjectives, therefore, British and UK mean the same. Great Britain, however, refers only to the mainland of England, Wales and Scotland.

Great Britain : England, Wales and Scotland. If you want to include Northern Ireland, use Britain or UK.

England : take care not to offend by saying England or English when you mean Britain or British.

Ulster : acceptable in headlines to mean Northern Ireland, which in fact comprises six of the nine counties of the province of Ulster.

Ireland : Irish Republic, not Eire.

So that is the guidance offered to Guardian journalists at the moment. We might argue furiously about these notes and, as usual, you will feel free to let me have your comments (I hope you will, because I would like to return to the subject).

The notes are not, we might as well admit, perfect. At least they represent an attempt to introduce some consistency into a fraught and changing situation in which our knowledge of history is too meagre to be of much help.

The Isles: A History, by Norman Davies, is, as a reader suggested, essential reading, discussing the naming of parts in their historical context. Davies remarks on the 'morass of mix-ups' and the 'number of citizens of the United Kingdom who do not appear to be familiar with the basic parameters of the state in which they live'.

He goes on: 'They often do not know what it is called; they do not distinguish between the whole and the constituent parts and they have never grasped the most elementary facts of its development. Confusion reigns on every hand.'

I could entertain you, or irritate you, for hours with examples from the Guardian. A note in the Guide not long ago under the heading Rock & Pop Music – Ireland... Dublin (nothing wrong so far) then called the event 'Rare UK date.' Last week we did it again to Cork. Perhaps this is the result of carrying news from the Republic of Ireland on our home news pages (I wrote about that in a column, Is Ireland too close to Home? February 28, 1998).

Ulster raises more serious complaints, such as one recently from an Irish reader who pointed out: 'I live in Ulster but not in Northern Ireland.' He lives in one of the three counties of Ulster that are in the Republic – but Ulster fits nicely in headlines (and N Ireland does not).

I will return to this. Meanwhile, here is a question to ask yourselves as you scan news in the Guardian about Ireland or various parts of the UK: do the terms we employ and the way we use them always clearly imply that we are relating to each other as equals? Does our loose way with terms mean that we simply do not care? Some of you do. I have files of complaints of affronted nationality and calls for fair play from readers all over the isles.

The Isles: A History by Norman Davies
is published in a revised paperback by Papermac.

The aftershock: our reaction to Tuesday's tragic events

→ 15 September 2001

The Guardian on Wednesday this week was an extraordinary one, reflecting the gravity of the unprecedented events in the United States. How well and appropriately it did it, and how it has performed in the days since then, is for you to judge.

More than 200,000 extra copies of Wednesday's paper were printed – a total of well over 600,000 – but even so, the demand for news proved to be greater than could be supplied.

Almost the first thing that the editor of the paper did as events unfolded on Tuesday lunchtime was to order the pre-print run of the Society section – then on the presses – to continue so that the larger circulation on Wednesday would be made up of complete copies containing all sections.

Several other decisions were made within the first hour as journalists clustered round the newsroom television sets. The size of the main broadsheet part of the paper, which was to have been 26 pages, was increased, first to 32 pages, but then as the magnitude of the catastrophe became clearer, to 36 pages.

The decision was taken to withhold all advertising from the main broadsheet news pages of the paper. Apart from the fact that the scale of the story clearly demanded extra space, it was judged that the juxtaposition of any advertising and the reports and pictures from the US would be completely inappropriate – a view shared by advertisers themselves, who began to ring in as the afternoon went on. On the comment pages, the diary was held over, partly to create more space, but again because of the content that those pages would clearly be carrying.

The decision was also taken to run the story continuously through the main paper rather than to divert any of it into a pull-out supplement. In the final editions it occupied the first 17 news pages, a further three city pages, the comment pages and the leading pages of G2, the tabloid second section.

While Wednesday's paper was being planned and staff who had been on leave or away from the office were converging on Farringdon Road, the news was already being carried on our website, Guardian Unlimited, where many of you will be reading this. At its peak, traffic on the website reached an unprecedented 146 page impressions a second. By the end of the day the total number of page impressions had reached 2.2m – twice the usual amount and higher than the previous daily peak of 1.7m, recorded the day after the last general election. The website would not have borne this weight of traffic without the radical restructuring that was completed only last month.

The technological context is important and relevant to the kind of paper the Guardian was able to deliver on Wednesday and subsequent days this week. All Guardian journalists now have a modern desktop computer on which they can monitor several wire services simultaneously while writing stories or laying out pages. Television and radio channels, too, will soon be distributed to desktop computers: the disaster in the United States coincided with a test to deliver CNN, the American 24-hour television news network, to selected desks in the Guardian newsroom.

Digital communications mean that both stories and pictures can now be filed within minutes of an event occurring, and subeditors can view all pictures coming in on the agency wires as well as those taken by the Guardian's own photographers.

The technology, however, does not determine the tone and quality of the content. The overwhelming desire around the paper on Tuesday was to produce a paper the appearance and content of which demonstrated that the enormity of what had happened had been apprehended and was being communicated as directly and forcefully as possible.

The first reaction to the news on Tuesday in the Guardian newsroom had been, as elsewhere, a stunned silence. Wednesday's paper opened, in effect, speechlessly. The front page in the final edition was entirely taken up with the unforgettable image of the twin towers of the World Trade Centre at the moment of the second impact. Pages two and three, a platform normally held by significant national and international stories, carried one picture across the entire two-page spread – a black and white image of Manhattan shrouded in billowing smoke.

Several of you objected to the inclusion among the comment pieces of an article by a writer on Muslim affairs relating Muslim terrorism to American foreign policy, at the very least as a premature and intrusive note.

But complaints, so far, have been few. Indeed, complaints about other things dropped suddenly and sharply after Tuesday. For the time being, at least, our priorities have changed.

News travels: a deluge of feedback from all over the world
→ 22 September 2001

Comment pieces in the Guardian in the immediate aftermath of the terrorist attacks on the World Trade Centre and the Pentagon, particularly those which argued a causal link between US foreign policy and the disaster, prompted an unprecedented mailbag from all over the world.

Letters to the editor almost doubled, reaching a peak on September 13 and 14 of well over 600 a day, most of them, of course, by email. That number is not, by itself, unprecedented. During the Gulf war a decade ago, before the establishment of our websites and before email, letters to the editor reached almost 900 a day, according to the person editing the letters page at that time.

What is unprecedented, it is safe to say, is the total volume of mail. Letters to Guardian Unlimited, our network of websites, roughly tripled in the immediate aftermath of the attack to peak at around 250 emails a day and email correspondence to individual writers has in some cases been huge.

One article, by the newly appointed editor of the Guardian's Comment pages, Seumas Milne, published on September 13 and headed 'They can't see why they are hated', attracted more than 2,000 emails directly to him and many more to other recipients in the Guardian.

A large number of those emails – but still a minority – were highly critical of the views expressed in the article. A few of them threatened the author with torture and mutilation. More reasonably, the main points of objection to this and other articles were that they were intrusive, insensitive and anti-American. The mildest critics argued that they were premature and that a decent interval should have been allowed before the struggle to analyse and understand began.

One email, referring specifically to the Milne article, concluded, 'The hatred felt towards Americans in his article made me want to vomit. By the way, I'm one of the nurses working on these patients. I'll be sure to tell the victims and their families that what happened was their fault, because they're Americans.'

The email response has provided a graphic reminder that writers in the Guardian no longer address only a generally sympathetic domestic constituency. The internet has changed all that. The editor in chief of Guardian Unlimited pointed out that beyond the Guardian's own website, news sources such as Yahoo and the search engine Google ensure that the Guardian's contents are available to a much wider audience than ever before. Syndication means that articles first published in the

Guardian are likely to appear in newspapers in many other parts of the world.

This wider audience, as the editor of Guardian Unlimited put it, does not necessarily share the paper's liberal principles and political orientation. As an illustration, she said that of the emails reaching her over the past week, the ratio of those criticising the Guardian's coverage to those commenting positively was about four to one. But among those writing from Britain the response was different, perhaps two to one in general agreement with the views expressed in pieces such as Milne's.

The letters editor says that the overwhelming majority of correspondence intended for his page is broadly supportive of the Guardian's coverage (to what extent the views of those who write to the letters page express those of the general readership of the paper we do not know).

To turn back to the 2,000 emails sent to Milne. We have not been able to read all of them, but we have sampled them at the beginning, when most of the letters were from readers in Britain, and at the end, after the lapse of a day or two, when far more people were writing from the US.

Of the first 250, roughly 25 percent were disagreeing with the views expressed in the piece, and 75 percent agreeing, at least to the extent that it was legitimate to propose a link between the attack and US foreign policy.

Towards the end, when far more Americans were making their views known the proportion had changed to almost 50–50 (130 people agreeing with Milne's views, 128 against, and another 100 commenting without either agreeing or disagreeing).

Many writers, from the US and elsewhere, have expressed their appreciation of the range of debate in the Guardian, not least for its inclusion of the Muslim writers whose opinions have been voiced. One British reader wrote, 'I hope the Guardian will continue to provide a forum for different opinions and world views. It is important to keep channels of communication and understanding open.'

I could not agree more.

Chain reaction: a reassessment of racial sensitivity
→ 29 September 2001

To say that we are living through a period of heightened sensitivity may seem the mildest understatement. At the time of writing, the Guardian is re-examining the language it uses in its coverage of the international crisis to try to avoid terms which may appear to imply that the paper equates terrorism with Islam. It does not.

However, as numerous readers testify, the paper does not always radiate great understanding of Islam. Several hundred readers complained, not always in the voice of moderation (and not all from the United Kingdom), about the view of Islam presented in a column by Julie Burchill, published in our Weekend magazine on August 18, well before the attack on the World Trade Centre. At her most reasonable, Ms Burchill summed up her opinions by saying, 'I believe that mindless, ill-sorted Islamophilia is just as dangerous as mindless, ill-sorted Islamophobia.'

More than half a dozen of you complained to the Press Complaints Commission, about the manner and content of the argument that led her to this conclusion. Although the PCC has not finished its consideration of all your complaints, it has already rejected most of them, broadly, in defence of freedom of speech. That is, it has defended Ms Burchill's right to her opinions, however outrageous we may consider them to be, and the paper's right to publish them. The key point is that Ms Burchill did not attack individuals. Had she done so, we may assume that the PCC code, with which the Guardian undertakes to comply, would have been contravened.

Paragraph 13 (i) on Discrimination reads, 'The press must avoid prejudicial or pejorative references to a *person's* [my italics] race, colour, religion, sex or sexual orientation or to any physical or mental illness or disability.'

Complaints about a subsequent column by Ms Burchill (September 22), in which she gave us her views on the German people, now also attracting a pained correspondence, would presumably fail for the same reason – that the Code allows strong and controversial general opinions to be expressed while drawing the line, in this context, at attacks on individuals.

What about the spirit of the Code? A German reader, living in the United Kingdom, asks a question of general relevance: 'How can a newspaper which portrays itself as liberal accept the explicit expression of discriminatory attitudes against a nation, playing on deeply entrenched stereotypes?'

It is a question that in my opinion the paper needs to consider more carefully. Would Julie Burchill's column on Islam have appeared had it been scheduled for publication after the attack on the World Trade Centre rather than before? Perhaps not, but what would you have called it had it been withheld in those circumstances – censorship or prudent editing?

Earlier this week our Middle East editor drew my attention to a guide published on the website of the Detroit Free Press (I give the address below) called '100 questions and answers about Arab Americans'. Its first aim is to inform the paper's own reporting (Detroit has 'the most concentrated' population of Arab Americans in the US). It was posted on the website this year before the present crisis in which it has acquired additional relevance as a modest counter to paranoia.

I can do no more than give a flavour of it here. It points out that the majority of the estimated three million Arab Americans were born in the United States, and then answers questions such as, Do Arabs have a shared religion? ('Most Arab Americans are Catholic or Orthodox Christians).' To which places do Arab Americans trace their ancestry? Is Palestine a country? What is the educational level of Arab Americans? and so on.

We have nothing like this answering questions, for example, about British Muslims, or about Islam, or the Arab world and, as your complaints remind us, we sometimes profess a knowledge which we do not possess. In our Education supplement this week, in a briefing about Bin Laden for 11- to 14-year-olds, we referred to 'the prophet Mohammed's tomb, the Ka'ba, in Mecca'. As the first of several correspondents (and not, I believe, a Muslim) pointed out, 'In fact, it is a shrine to God, and pre-dates Mohammed, having been established according to tradition by Abraham. This misdescription might give offence to Muslims, as implicitly reviving the medieval falsehood that Muslims worship Mohammed.'

We shall continue to try to correct our mistakes as we go, but should we at the same time be doing more to counter prejudice and less to reinforce it?

www.freep.com/jobspage/arabs.htm

T-shirt test: a correction we shouldn't have made
→ 06 October 2001

On Tuesday September 11, the day on which our priorities changed dramatically and complaints to my office dropped to practically nothing from the record level at which they had been running, we carried a correction that has proved to be unusually contentious. Indeed the question that subsequent developments have raised is: should the correction have been carried at all? Certainly had I known what I know now it would not have appeared.

The correction concerned Dr David Hoile, the director of the European-Sudanese Public Affairs Council (Espac). Dr Hoile had been the subject of three items in the Guardian Diary up to that time. A further item appeared in the Diary on the day that the correction appeared. At the time of writing, eight more have appeared – suggesting perhaps that corrections, far from suppressing inquiry, sometimes stimulate it.

The main question the Diary was asking was whether Dr Hoile had, in his student days in the 1980s, when he was associated with the Federation of Conservative Students, worn a 'badge or T-shirt' (Diary, August 30) carrying the slogan 'Hang Mandela'. The Diary made several appeals to readers for photographic evidence that would prove the point.

On September 6, Dr Hoile complained by fax to the editor of the Diary, to the editor of the Guardian and to me about 'misreporting' on several points and requesting 'corrections and clarifications'. Dr Hoile was adamant in his rebuttal of any suggestion that he had ever worn a T-shirt carrying the slogan 'Hang Mandela' or anything like it.

In one of several telephone conversations I warned Dr Hoile against pursuing a correction that might subsequently be found to be false. Dr Hoile told me there was absolutely no chance of that happening and insisted that no such T-shirt had existed.

He advised me to talk to a journalist who had been closely following his activities and those of the Federation of Conservative Students at the time. I did that and the journalist told me, 'I never saw him or anyone else wearing a [Hang] Nelson Mandela T-shirt.'

After discussions with the Diary and others, I concluded that there were minor inaccuracies and that there was no convincing evidence that Dr Hoile had worn a Hang Mandela T-shirt.

This remained the position four days after Dr Hoile had made his original complaint to me and on September 11, the following correction appeared: 'References to David Hoile in several recent Diary items have suggested that he is currently a researcher for the Conservative MP

Andrew Hunter. Dr Hoile tells us categorically that he is not and we accept that. There is no evidence that Dr Hoile ever wore a "Hang Mandela" T-shirt, or that he possessed or borrowed a rottweiler. Furthermore, Dr Hoile wishes to say equally categorically that at no time did he propose a motion at Warwick University that "Nelson Mandela is a terrorist and should be hanged" nor would he have done so. The Guardian has no evidence for that either.'

Immediately after the publication of this correction, the Diary was held out for a week because the page on which it normally appeared was accommodating more material relating to the terrorist attack on the World Trade Centre and the Pentagon.

In the interim, the Diary did indeed obtain a photograph of Dr Hoile, the publication of which it began to trail in Diary items, referring now to his denial of ever having worn 'Hang Mandela accoutrements' (September 20), or 'paraphernalia' (September 25). It published on September 26 what it presented as a picture of Dr Hoile wearing his 'Hang Mandela kit' – in the form of a sticker attached to his tie.

I rang up Dr Hoile on the day of publication and suggested that he owed the Guardian an apology. Dr Hoile apologised profusely to me for any 'embarrassment' he had caused me personally. He insisted, however, that word for word, the correction remained correct. He had absolutely no recollection of wearing anything of the kind shown in the photograph, but he had known beyond any doubt that he had not worn a Hang Mandela T-shirt.

There are several things to be said here. The first is to assert the principle that it is better to have conclusive evidence before rather than after serious allegations are made. Minor errors render serious arguments vulnerable to doubt. But the equally important point is that when a sentiment such as Hang Mandela is expressed, the precise nature of the vehicle on which it is carried is not the main thing.

Dr Hoile does not seem to be quite ready to concede the point. For my part, I am ready to say to the editor of the Diary and his colleagues, that on the main issue, you were right.

Worlds apart: the international appeal of the website
→ 13 October 2001

Three weeks ago I wrote about your response to the Guardian's coverage of the terrorist attacks on the US and their aftermath, pointing out the huge increase in demand for news and analysis not just from within the United Kingdom but from all over the world through our network of websites.

In normal times 60 percent or a little over, of those of you who read the Guardian online do so from the UK and 40 per cent from other parts of the world. The precise statistics, from the last survey are: 62 per cent UK 13 per cent other European countries, 12 per cent US and 13 per cent other parts of the world.

These figures, however, date from May this year and the new ones which will result from a survey beginning on Monday are likely to show a significant difference, particularly in the number using the website from the US. Our calculations suggest we now have more than half a million regular readers in the US.

The use of the website in September was unprecedented, with 44m page impressions – an increase on our main news site of 74 per cent – and 3.7m 'unique users', individuals counted once no matter how many times they used the site during the month. As many as 14 per cent of those may have been in the US.

In my earlier column (September 22) I wrote that this wider audience did not necessarily share the paper's liberal principles. I dwelt rather on the adverse criticism that our coverage attracted, especially when critical of US foreign policy or providing a platform for voices from the Muslim world.

It is just this breadth of coverage, however, that many of you outside the UK, including many Americans, have been turning to the website for. Let me quote one or two of you who felt that the Guardian was providing a range of comment unavailable in your own media. From Massachusetts: 'I am an American who fears, more than any terrorist, the apparently fierce determination among many Americans to remain ignorant about what lay behind this tragedy . . .'; from Hawaii: 'You have somehow escaped the biases of the American press . . .'; from New York: 'You help me sift through the smoke and soot fanned by America's media, their shrill jingoism, and [help me] to preserve my sanity'; from Los Angeles: 'Most of the US media tends to be rather shallow . . . word of mouth has a fair number of people who work for the film studios here perusing your site.' I have a great many more similar emails, not all from the US – from Canada, Mexico, Japan, Australia (a reader who complained of being Murdochised), Germany, Italy.

Some readers who clearly visited the site for coverage of the crisis wrote in praise of other things they found there. One reader particularly appreciated our coverage of religious affairs and the weekly Face to Faith articles: 'I live in a very small town in Kentucky, surrounded by radical fundamentalism. There is absolutely no one here to talk with about such modern ideas and interpretations.'

We have yet to appreciate the full significance to the paper of this great extension of the Guardian's readership, a readership able to receive the news and make its views felt immediately. At present those of you visiting the site have little indication that you are part of this international community of readers.

A sprinkling of your comments finds its way into the letters page of the main paper (which is also available on the website), while many of your emails are circulated to relevant individual correspondents and editors. But, apart from the talkboards, which do not always sustain their discussions at, let us say, the highest level, there is no website forum for your views comparable with the paper's greatly oversubscribed letters page. Letters from website users outside the UK represent a resource of potentially great value and interest which is at present untapped.

The editor-in-chief of Guardian Unlimited says that on her appointment before the present crisis, she perceived the absence of such a forum as a gap and is in the process of changing the situation. By early next year your views should have proper representation there. 'We want to show that you can get intelligent debate on a website,' she says.*

The editor of the Guardian says he is all for that. He does not see the huge email response from beyond the UK as a pressure on the paper or its liberal values, and certainly not a threat to them. It demonstrates, he says, that the widest possible selection of views which the Guardian disseminates is being amplified throughout the world. 'Many Arabs and Muslims are astonished at what they read. I love that thought.'

A final word from the editor: 'I suppose that once you are aware of this international dimension you can't help but think a little more internationally and be a little less anglocentric.'

Plans to introduce such a feature have still not materialised.

Leading lights: deciding the editorial line on Afghanistan

→ 20 October 2001

This week began with a flurry of calls demanding, not unreasonably, to know why the anti-war march in London last weekend was not covered in Monday's Guardian. The most modest estimate of numbers put the size of the march at 20,000 and the organisers believed that as many as 50,000 people had turned out. It was covered in our sister paper the Observer on Sunday with a picture and accompanying story, but, most of us would agree, not exhaustively.

I raised the matter at the first opportunity, the editor's Monday morning conference which, since September 11, has been attended by up to 60 members of the editorial staff of the paper. The editor's immediate response was to say that he agreed with the callers, it was a mistake and should have been covered.

It is the paper's general policy not to cover marches.* The editor said that in the present context this case was clearly different. He added that 20,000 people – among them many Muslims – most of them possibly 'Guardian readers', as he put it, had been on the march and we had appeared not to notice.

Let us come back to the paper's leader line, which has not been against the military action but offering qualified support for it. It may be that the paper is passing through one of the defining periods of its history. The editor points to the access the paper is providing to a range of opinion that is not generally available and that has been gaining readers via the website in the US but also in the Arab and Muslim worlds and elsewhere (I wrote about this in more detail in my column last week).

What the editor actually said was that the Guardian may be passing through a defining moment like Suez. In fact, at the time of Suez, the Guardian (and the Observer), amid the general jingoism, conspicuously stood against the invasion. One or two of the leader writers believe that that is what the paper should be doing now, calling for an end to military action which it should not have supported in the first place. That is a minority view.

What the paper has done, very carefully since September 11, is to offer its support for military action on the understanding that it is accompanied by continuing diplomatic and humanitarian efforts, placing itself, perhaps, where it is best able to exert influence on the government. That, the editor says, is what the Guardian signed up to.

On more than one occasion in the past few weeks, the leader writers have reminded themselves that if influence is to be exerted then the effort is better directed at the British government rather than at

Washington. One leader writer invoked the Skibbereen Eagle in support of this argument. That was the small newspaper in West Cork that warned the Tsar of Russia against his expansionist designs on China, saying it, the Skibbereen Eagle, had its eye on him. It is used as a call to reality (and a guard against portentousness which the Guardian leaders seem to be free from).

I have been attending the meetings of the leader writers this week, chaired on all but one occasion by the editor. I prepared myself by reading or re-reading chronologically all the Guardian editorials on the crisis since September 12. Of many worth re-reading I would particularly mention that of October 11, The roots of the rage: Islam and the west must also look inwards. You might conclude that the paper is fortunate in the experience that congregates in its leader room at present.

That is not to say that the collective view is always arrived at in an atmosphere of unbroken calm. The debate was particularly lively in the middle of this week. On Wednesday the leader writers considered what the options were in the light of increasingly ominous warnings of the growing human tragedy for the Afghan people. One question considered, among a range of others, was whether calling for a pause in the bombing to facilitate relief efforts would be consistent with support for a continuation of the war by other means. Would it, in practical terms, assist the relief effort? Would it give the Taliban time to regroup and redeploy? In the end this debate was overtaken by the growing importance of the anthrax story in the US and it was this that formed the subject of the leader in Thursday's paper.

The argument that prevailed when yesterday's leader came up for discussion was one urging a call for humanitarian aid to be given much greater priority as the military and diplomatic operations continued.

One final point. There is a distinction between the views debated in the pages of the paper and those that appear in the leader columns. In the latter you hear the voice of the Guardian, although you do not have to agree with what it is saying.

See the next article: Out of step

Out of step: marches and other conspiracies
→ 27 October 2001

The statement, or misstatement, in this column last week that, to quote myself, 'It is the paper's general policy not to cover marches' caused an angry response from readers, whose views were made clear on Monday's letters page. The editor appeared at my door quite early on Monday to say that the 'policy' had come as something of a surprise to him and that he would like to offer a calming and clarifying note for Tuesday's corrections column.

Since I know that many of you who read this column on Saturdays are not attentive readers of the daily corrections column, this is what he said: 'It is not correct to state that it is our general policy not to cover marches or demonstrations. The news desk forms a judgment about such events, based on a number of factors, including timing, topicality and size. We have covered several demonstrations over the past year. Demonstrations on Saturdays would normally be covered in Sunday newspapers, but there are exceptional circumstances when Guardian reporters would be present.'

In a personal response to some of those who protested he repeated what I had reported in last week's column, that the march of October 13 should have been covered. 'Not to have covered that march adequately was our mistake.' His letter to readers ended, 'Please be assured that we do not have a blanket policy either in favour of covering demonstrations, or against covering them.' (The march was, in fact, covered throughout October 13 on our website, last updated at 6.15 that evening.)

Apropos the statement that caused the controversy, I will just say, while readily conceding that it did not come from the lips of the editor, that I do not get my news from nowhere. I drew the wrong conclusion from my conversations on the subject around the Guardian.

One senior journalist, discovering a charity that I had hardly suspected, said that the argument had served the useful purpose of focusing attention on the issue of marches and providing not only readers, but the paper's journalists with a clearer view of its policy.

One of the more telling points made by readers between the publication of my article and the appearance of the editor's note was that not to cover peaceful marches helped to reinforce the view of those who felt that violence paid.

In passing, perhaps, I should mention without comment that there were a couple of letters such as this one: 'Whilst I respect the right of 20,000 to march in London, let us keep things in perspective. The government should not necessarily give in to the demands of the most vocal

0.03 per cent of the population.'

There are, and there always will be, readers who will not believe us when we say we made a mistake, an error of judgment, or that we decided to do one thing instead of another. 'You expect us to believe this was a "mistake"? I'm sorry, but that is just not credible. If that is what you were told then it is an absolute whopping lie. . . . Guardian readers were led to believe that you are the readers' editor, not the editor's messenger.'

I believe that it is to our mutual benefit that I try to encourage a critical view of the paper based on as much information as possible about the way it actually works – and stumbles – rather than the way you may think it works. I shall keep trying.

Another reader, a teacher, has been in touch with me over the past week to know why the reported 'death' of Mullah Omar's young son ranked only a sentence or two on page two on Monday. This reader had written without success to the letters page in these terms: 'Why was the atrocity not front-page news? Why was there no sense of outrage? Why the silence? Did you somehow miss this or do you just not care? Sorry, for a moment I thought you were a newspaper whose job it is to report the news.' I have tried to assist, particularly since the subject is to be discussed in class and I have been warned that my response or lack of it will be telling.

The teacher's interest was stimulated by a note embedded in a report from Islamabad, page two, October 22, in which we said that a doctor had confirmed to the BBC that Mullah Omar's son had been killed in air strikes.

But had he? Our correspondents in northern Afghanistan and in Islamabad could not confirm it. The foreign desk here in Farringdon Road recalled carrying the report on a previous occasion (page one, October 12). Reuters mentioned it in a dispatch on October 17. On October 22 AP quoted the Taliban strongly denying that Mullah Omar's son had been killed. 'It is completely false. His son is fine. Mullah Omar is fine. Osama is fine. His bases are fine. Our morale is high.' We did not carry that. Perhaps we should have done. It is difficult to know what to believe. You choose.

Mortal wound: respect – or otherwise – for the dead
→ 03 November 2001

The obituaries page of the Guardian, which I edited before moving to this job (moving, as a colleague said at the time, from the dead to the injured), has never presumed to offer a last judgment on its tenants. They lie there side by side, of all classes, creeds, nationalities and races. No more is asked of them than that they are dead and that in life they achieved a degree of fame or notoriety.

The obituary may be affectionate or, in some circumstances, acerbic, and in most cases is somewhere in between. That it is not meant to be the last word is shown by the readiness with which the page finds room for letters of comment. These often add something that the obituarist missed or could not have known, or they object, sometimes most strongly, to the assessment of the person obituarised.

The regular appearance of such letters is a unique feature of the Guardian obituaries page. More than 70 have appeared on the page since the beginning of April this year. Among those published recently were several taking issue with the obituary (September 26) of the Labour politician Peter Shore. The obituary itself, elegantly written by a very experienced political commentator, was, depending on your point of view, uncompromisingly frank, or, to quote one who wrote in protest, 'vindictive and petty'.

I do not wish to renew the distress it caused, but the opening sentence set the tone for what followed. It began, 'No political career could be sadder than that of a man who, having leapfrogged into the cabinet over the ministers of state above him, is, 20 years later, voted "the 12th most effective backbencher".'

One friend of Shore wrote to protest that 'the man described . . . is barely recognisable as the one I had the privilege of knowing throughout such a long period'. He objected that the writer had failed to fulfil what he called the 'overriding responsibility' to (I paraphrase) convey a sense of the whole man.

His reaction and that of others raise questions which are often raised for the journalists who work on this page. How frank should an obituary be? To what extent should the feelings of friends, and particularly relatives, be considered? To what extent should the speed with which the obituary follows the death of its subject be an inhibition? To what extent does the licence to be frank depend on how well the obituarist knew his subject? Can the obituary of a public figure be more forthright than that of someone whose career was pursued out of the public eye? In what circumstances should an obituary take advantage of the fact that the dead cannot be libelled? And so on.

The words of CP Scott, the author of our ethos, come to mind. After his famous remark, 'Comment is free, but facts are sacred', he went on to say something that is perhaps too little remembered: 'Comment also is justly subject to a self-imposed restraint. It is well to be frank it is even better to be fair.'

Most of the time the publication of a letter on the page will help when an obituary has caused offence. Recently, and unusually, it was the letter, and not the obituary on which it was commenting – that of the historian JH Plumb – that brought protests. The obituarist, in the context of a whole-page notice, had referred to Professor Plumb's 'colourful character' and to his reputation as 'the rudest man in Cambridge'. No one objected to this since the qualities and achievements and charities of the professor were properly placed before us.

The writer of the letter (with the approval of the page editor, who agreed to publish) thought that what was lacking was a specific example of Professor Plumb's volatility. He proceeded to relate an incident in which he had been personally involved, in which the professor had, let us just say, blown up. The objectors felt that it was offensive, smacked of scoresettling and should not have been published. They were probably right, and the editors of the obituaries page have now been asked by the editor of the paper to consider pejorative elements in obituaries and letters more carefully.

Recently a complaint was made, not that the subject of an obituary had been unfairly treated, but that a dead member of the family had in a passing reference been described in unacceptable and offensive terms. I concluded that in this case the publication of a corrective letter would have been a reasonable resolution of the complaint. The Guardian's external ombudsman and the Press Complaints Commission agreed with that adjudication when the complaint was pursued, in turn, with them. The complainants remain unsatisfied.

It is not an easy page to edit.

Incorrigible?: the rights and wrongs of daily journalism
→ 10 November 2001

It is not something to boast about, but we have published a record number of items in the daily corrections and clarifications column during the past year – the fourth full year since my appointment in November 1997. (This is my annual report.) The new year began on November 5, marked by the usual celebrations throughout the land.

I know you like to be precise, so the precise figure was roughly 1,517 – 85 more than the previous year. In fact, the figure has risen each year since I began, although the ratio of calls (emails, telephone calls, letters, faxes) to corrections has remained remarkably constant at between four and five to one. It was five to one over the past year. That rate is slightly better than it appears to be because quite often many of you complain about the same thing. Some calls are not seeking corrections. And some complaints are rejected – forgive me for pointing it out – because you are wrong and the journalist is right.

I do not think the annual increase in the number of errors corrected necessarily represents an increase in the number of errors – I almost said sins – committed. I think it represents – although I do not wish to take too much credit – my own and my assistant's gradual scaling of the heights of human capability. With oxygen we might succeed in going farther, but I suspect that we have reached a plateau and must, in a rather uncomfortable way, be content.

I have no precise or even rough idea of how many errors go unnoticed and uncorrected, but I believe that it is probably quite as many again as we actually correct. I have taken several opportunities in the past four years to say precisely that – on the principle that it is well to be frank, but also for self-preservation. We have never claimed to correct everything, and I say it once more in the faint hope that those of you who pursue a minor point, sometimes with alarming fervour down the weeks and months, will, so to speak, take the point.

A sense of perspective and proportion is important. It is not a complacency to remind ourselves now and again that the corrections stand on the main body of the Guardian as a tick stands on the back of a large horse (perhaps causing it to frisk occasionally).

No human being is able to read and to comprehend fast enough to keep pace with the outpourings of the Guardian. As the paper's features editor, Ian Katz, points out in his introduction to the forthcoming Guardian Year 2001, an average word count for the daily edition of the paper has lately been about 250,000 words, and on a Saturday this rises to 400,000. One day's paper, even on a weekday, may be the equivalent to the combined bulk of, say, Gulliver's Travels, The Jungle Book, The Wind in the Willows and The Wizard of Oz (titles chosen because they are handy for an electronic count).

In one of our more productive weeks – to give an idea of the impossibility of the challenge presented to the reader who is determined to read the lot – we produce something almost three times the length of War and Peace. I am not presenting bulk as an essential virtue, before those of you who write to me to complain of the waste of paper write again, but simply as a fact.

The events of September 11 and the aftermath – a word that a former editor of the paper, Alastair Hetherington, once advised his staff was to be used only in its proper sense of 'second mowing' – quelled among readers of the Guardian their normal will to complain about minor matters. Calls plummeted to half their usual level, and so did corrections. It took a month for them to return to the high rate at which they had been running. They are now quite as they were before the terrorist attacks. We are looking, I think, at the heroic persistence of pedantry in the face of adversity.

Accompanying the dramatic fall in complaints after September 11 was a huge surge in the demand for news and comment, reflected in a jump in circulation and readership of the printed paper and a positive leap in use of the website, Guardian Unlimited. A year ago, in October 2000, the website had 1.4m users. Last month the figure was 5.1m, recording 53.5m page impressions.

It does not take long for readers to develop high expectations of the Guardian, and sometimes they are not fulfilled. I pointed to the number of corrections the Guardian carries when a reader this week asked me whether complaining had any effect. Corrections, he replied, were an indicator of failure. No they are not, but failing to make them would be.

News clash: tough decisions as two stories break at once
→ 17 November 2001

The paper of Tuesday this week was in some ways a particularly chal-
lenging one to produce, calling for a running evaluation of two
competing – and for some time, it was thought, connected – stories: the
rapid advance of the Northern Alliance across Afghanistan, and the
crash of the Airbus in New York.

The dilemma posed by the New York crash was summed up in the
Austin cartoon which appeared on the front page in all editions, a plume
of smoke in the form of a question mark rising from the crashed airliner. Was it or was it not an act of terrorism?

This was the question that through the day dominated the thinking
about the crash and the way it was to be treated, not only on the news
pages of the paper but also on the comment and analysis pages. As the
hours passed the probability that it was an accident rather than a terrorist act increased but it was not a question likely to be answered
conclusively as that night's deadlines came and went.

Clearly, even if it were not terrorism, the coverage had to reflect the
seriousness of an air crash in which some 260 people, most of them from
the Dominican Republic, were killed that the crash had happened in a
city still struggling to come to terms with September 11, that it had
crashed in a district where many of the victims of the terrorist attack had
had their homes. But how much space to give it in the paper?

At the same time the pace of events in Afghanistan was surprising
everyone, and that story needed constant attention and updating, which
it received for the last time that night at about 3.30am on Tuesday. Then
a slip edition – for which the presses are stopped briefly in the course of
a run to allow limited changes to be made – was put out, with 60,000
copies being printed on the presses in London and 20,000 on those at
Trafford Park, Manchester.

The main headline on the front page remained the same (although
changes were made to the text): 'The day disaster returned to the streets
of New York'. The heading originally stripped across the page beneath it
was 'Northern Alliance at the gates of Kabul'. That ran until the 3.30am
slip edition, when it became 'Northern Alliance enters Kabul as Taliban
flee'.

Page five, the first or 'front page' of six devoted to, as the folio line
termed it, Attack on Afghanistan, was slipped at 3.30am too. That had
been carrying a headline 'Alliance fights to within a few miles of Kabul
as Taliban flee shattered city'. For the final 80,000 copies of the night it
became 'Northern Alliance takes control of Kabul as Taliban troops flee'

above a substantially rewritten report.

So in Tuesday's paper, the crash dominated the front and then ran for a further three pages inside. The developments in Afghanistan ran at the foot of the front and then from pages five to 10 inside.

No other news appeared in the paper until page 11, the first page of national news. Did we get that right? On Wednesday we carried among the letters to the editor one questioning the scale of values that devoted four pages to a crash in which about 260 people had been killed and a mere paragraph on page 15 to floods in Algeria which had claimed 575 lives. The floods, at the time of writing, had received scant coverage in the Guardian. Should that story have displaced more space in Tuesday's paper? What factors should be considered when decisions of this kind are being made? We might come back to the relativity of news on another occasion.

The floods received rather more coverage on our website, Guardian Unlimited, where there are no constraints of space. The website also dealt with the crash as its lead story, with the advantage, of course, that it could treat that and the events in Afghanistan as breaking news, giving its users immediate access to the available information. A message thread also ran on the website with users from the United Kingdom and elsewhere seeking and exchanging news about the crash – a demonstration of the anxiety and urgency of the demand that runs ahead of provision in these circumstances.

To return to the paper, the uncertainties of two major developing stories posed problems for the comment and analysis pages. One of the columns that was held out was about the crisis in the airline industry, a subject agreed between the writer and the editor of the section the previous Sunday. If anything, it became more relevant, but it was considered, rightly, that it would have been insensitive to use it on Tuesday.

One senior columnist was asked to write a contingency piece against any revelation that the crash was after all caused by an act of terrorism. She filed that at 7.30pm. At 8pm on Monday, that was held too.

Drawn apart: keeping Hitler out of the picture

→ 24 November 2001

A few weeks ago we carried a substantial article headed 'Sketch poser from artist who snubbed Hitler: drawing of Führer casts new light on tale of heroic stand'. It brought a swift request from the son of the artist that we should make it clear, first of all, that his father never met Hitler, and secondly, that he never wavered in his anti-Nazi stance. The artist's son believed that our report suggested the opposite and he demanded an apology.

The report that brought this strong objection referred to a retro-spective exhibition in Leicester, which has now ended, devoted to the work of a German artist, Johannes Matthaeus Koelz. Koelz fled Germany in 1937 and died in Stoke-on-Trent in 1971. The story appeared in the Guardian on October 6 and mentioned a documentary, not yet broadcast, called – 'actually called', our report said – The Man Who Wouldn't Paint Hitler, a title emphasising Koelz's avowedly anti-Nazi beliefs.

On December 28 last year the Guardian had published an article about Koelz, across the full width of a broadsheet news page, beneath the heading 'Artistic act of bravery pieced together'. It was, in effect, a scene-setter for the Leicester exhibition which was to contain the reassembled fragments of Koelz's masterpiece, an anti-war triptych called Thou Shalt Not Kill.

To quote from that report: 'Koelz, who won the Iron Cross for his courage in the first world war, was forced to flee Germany after refusing to paint Hitler's portrait in 1937. He was given 48 hours' warning of his impending arrest, and before he fled he cut his greatest work, a monu-mental triptych, into 25 pieces.'

When the Leicester exhibition – a tribute to the labours over many years of Koelz's daughter, Ava Farrington – opened at the beginning of March this year, it contained those pieces of the triptych that had been found, but most surprisingly, a photograph of a drawing by Koelz, appar-ently made in 1936, of Adolf Hitler. The drawing was discovered by Mrs Farrington in a private collection in Germany. The photograph of it was included in both the exhibition and the catalogue, captioned without further comment 'Sketch portrait of Hitler, 1936'.

However, the catalogue does say this about the period from which the drawing dates, a time when Koelz's outspoken views were beginning to get him into trouble: 'Summoned to court to answer a charge of "insulting the Fuhrer", [Koelz] found himself in front of a judge whose hobby was painting and who "allowed me to talk myself out of the situation I had talked myself into".'

'That summer, [Gauleiter Wagner, the provincial governor, arrived at Koelz's home] to offer a commission – a portrait of Hitler for reproduction as a title page in a propaganda publication. A great honour and a seductive fee also, perhaps, an attempt to persuade this difficult but very talented artist into the Nazi fold. But a condition of the commission was that Koelz should wear the brown shirt of the Nazi party for the eight planned sittings.'

The catalogue note says that Koelz was appalled, and quotes from his own record: 'I could not see myself . . . a writer and artist who had committed himself to democratic ideals. . . . identifying myself visibly with a crowd of adolescent hooligans and nitwits. . . . I refused politely, but firmly.'

Shortly after this encounter Koelz left Germany with his wife, their baby daughter, now Mrs Farrington, and their teenage son, Siegfried, who now complains that the Guardian has maligned his father by questioning his attitude towards Hitler.

In the article of October 6, we said that Ava Farrington was convinced that, had her father ever met Hitler, he would have told her. She believed the drawing was made from a photograph. Siegfried, during one of several conversations I have had with him, made the same point. He also confessed to some bitterness that his father, after the dangers in which his anti-Nazi beliefs had placed him in Germany, was interned on reaching Britain and then sent to Australia. Siegfried is, he said, sensitive to the slightest disparagement of his father.

To return to his complaint, there may be a mystery over the precise circumstances in which the drawing was made. There is no evidence that it was the result of a meeting or sitting. The drawing itself does not constitute it. Nor is there any evidence that it represents a wobble in Koelz's beliefs. Indeed, everything that is known about Koelz suggests the contrary.

The exhibition received a record number of visitors, more than 30,000. Not one, in the notes in the visitors' books, found anything ambivalent in Koelz's position. Nor should anyone have done in the Guardian pieces.

Snap judgment: pictures of children used without permission

→ 12 January 2002

On two occasions recently the Guardian has published pictures of young people which have drawn justified complaints from parents. The point about both was not that the pictures in themselves had anything wrong with them. They were the kind of photographs that, in different circumstances, the parents who complained might have been pleased to see. The objections were prompted largely by the context in which they were used.

The first picture, which appeared in the paper's Society section last November 28, showed three girls running past a community centre in Oldham. The context was a visit to the centre by the chairman of the Oldham independent review looking into riots in the town and prevailing racial attitudes.

The mother of one girl had already refused permission for her daughter to be interviewed by television in connection with the visit. She was more than a little upset to discover the Guardian picture. She felt that the headline, quoting the words of an Asian youth from a nearby part of Oldham, 'If you go into a white area you are only going to get abuse', suggested that her daughter and her two friends – all 12 years of age, all white, and all readily recognisable – held racist and specifically anti-Asian prejudices, and this, she said, was certainly not the case. No permission was sought before the picture was taken.

I felt that the objections raised and the anxieties that were voiced were reasonable and might have been anticipated and I said that the picture should not have been used.

I feel much the same about the second case. This involved a picture used in a two-page spread in G2 on December 17, in which a staff journalist looked at racial attitudes in Leeds in the context of the attack on an Asian student by a group that included a Leeds United footballer.

Three pictures were used. On the left-hand page there were two small ones in black and white, showing Sarfraz Najeib, the person who was attacked, and Jonathan Woodgate, the Leeds footballer who was found guilty of affray. Almost half the area of the right-hand page was taken up by a colour photograph of an unidentified young Asian in medium close-up looking straight out at the reader. No other face was visible in the picture. The caption read, 'In the crowd . . . a Leeds fan at Elland Road. Supporters are bewildered that their club is once again being associated with racism.'

This picture was taken with a long lens. The photographer did not seek permission and the boy in the picture was unaware that it had been taken. His father – the family are Hindu – who was actually with his son at the match, objected strongly. He felt that the picture had unacceptably raised his son, who was 14 at the time, to uncomfortable prominence in the midst of a controversial situation and in a way that was clearly likely to induce anxieties. He thought this should have been anticipated, particularly, as he put it, by a paper such as the Guardian.

I agree with him. Although the paper was acting with positive intent and the picture was chosen to show that Asians were continuing to enjoy Leeds matches, it was unfair to nominate a single young individual to make this point. At my request the editor asked for the picture to be deleted from our archive.

I thought it would be useful to hear the views of the boy, so with the agreement of his father, I visited him at his home in West Yorkshire. He said he was at school when the paper was pointed out to him by a succession of three teachers, one of whom gave him a pass to go out and get a copy of the paper for himself. His first thought, he said, was 'Wow! my picture in the paper.' Then some of his friends, many of whom are Muslims, started taunting him as Leeds United's 'token Asian'. He went through the day feeling uncomfortable and vulnerable, and, by the time he got home that evening to talk to his father about it, he was angry. He stayed away from the next Leeds home match. 'I am just someone who likes football and likes watching Leeds. I don't think of myself as "a Leeds United fan".'

The code of the Press Complaints Commission is not totally helpful. The use of the long lens is not relevant since its restriction applies to private places or public places where there is a reasonable expectation of privacy. A football queue is not such a place. But the code also says: 'Journalists must not interview or photograph children under the age of 16 on subjects involving the welfare of the child . . . in the absence of or without the consent of a parent [or responsible adult].' The phrase 'the welfare of the child' needs clarifying. However the intention is clear enough. In both these cases the paper should have thought a bit more about the burden it was imposing.

Heads you win: the art of the headline writer
→ 26 January 2002

Headlines attract a lot of attention, a statement I feel fairly safe in making. I am sure the subeditor who wrote the headline, in a paper in the US, 'War dims hope for peace,' must have felt the same way. They represent that area of our endeavours where our talents are most obviously exposed to instant praise or ridicule.

Slip up in a headline and hostilities break out immediately, usually between the paper and its readers but sometimes between the author of the piece and the person who wrote the headline misconstruing it. Skirmishes in the latter category are conducted in the knowledge that many readers have a misconception that the person who writes the report and the journalist who puts the headline on it are one and the same. They almost never are.

The best headlines achieve a long afterlife. When I asked colleagues around the office to nominate a favourite, the one that came up most frequently was (not from the Guardian), Book lack in Ongar – on a report about a crisis in the library service in Essex. (For the benefit of English-language students at the international school in Frankfurt, whose teacher asked for a glossary of headline puns, this one is a play – no pun intended – on the title of John Osborne's Look Back in Anger.)

Some of the most famous headlines have been contributed to the pantheon unwittingly. It seems a pity that the author of the wartime headline 'French push bottles up German rear' remains anonymous.

Harold Evans in his book News Headlines (Heinemann, 1974), said good headlines should be self-contained telegrams. 'Simplicity, informality and impact are the essence. . . . It must be a clear signal swiftly readable, economical in editorial, production, and reading time, and in newsprint space proportionate to the news and flexible.'

Headlines are not an uncommon source of complaint, even when they induce the flicker of a smile. Our treatment of a recent disaster brought this email: 'May I add my name to the list of those who would have wanted to congratulate the Guardian headline writer on Saturday? "2000 dead – and rising" lifted my day. Should have been kept for an edition closer to Easter!'

Most of the serious complaints about headlines are to do with exaggeration or with the statement as fact of something not supported by the text. For a number of readers, our front-page lead last Saturday fell into the latter category. The headline said: 'Saudis tell US forces to get out'. One reader complained, 'Nowhere in the article does the author actually support this statement. In fact, the article does state that "Both sides have been desperately denying for months that there is a rift". I think this reader, and others who wrote similarly, have a point, although the journalist who wrote the report had no problem with the headline.

On headline hyperbole, another reader wrote, 'I am becoming increasingly concerned at the number of Guardian headlines which report someone's "fury" at an event rather than the event itself. A good example being "Blunkett fury at asylum camp defeat". . . . This seems to be an old tabloid trick when "Anger at . . ." became just too dull.'

To return to Harold Evans. He points out that the Press Council, the forerunner of the Press Complaints Commission, 'rightly upheld complaints [in the 1960s] where mild criticism has been headlined "slammed" or "lashed". It has insisted that a headline should be wholly true to the purport of the text and not merely to part of it.'

The best headlines encourage the false impression that they are all easily arrived at. Apart from the requirements already mentioned, they have to fit a specific column width in a certain fount and size of type. They have to indicate the relative importance of the content in relation to the other news on the page. And they are almost always written under pressure.

One colleague, pushed to explain his craft, devised the following, with apologies to Andrew Marvell: 'Had we but world enough and time/ This headline, laddie, were no crime.'

To reward headline-writing skills, the assistant editor (production) recently introduced a monthly competition within the Guardian. The first 'headline of the year' – judged by the managing director – has just been chosen. She picked one by Julie Reid, the chief subeditor of G2, put on a story about musicians who defied the Taliban. It said, simply and aptly: 'The banned played on'.

I leave you with a favourite, reproduced in a book by Fritz Spiegl, What The Papers Didn't Mean to Say, published by his Scouse Press, Liverpool, in 1965. The first deck said: 'Sibelius dies'. The second deck said: 'as he hears Sargent conducting his Fifth Symphony'. More later, perhaps.

Words' worth: saying what we mean and meaning what we say

→ 16 February 2002

I am often reminded of Alice or, more specifically, of her encounter with Humpty Dumpty in chapter six of Through The Looking-Glass (And what Alice found there). 'When I use a word,' Humpty Dumpty said, in rather a scornful tone, 'it means just what I choose it to mean – neither more nor less.'

Some of those who write for the Guardian take this Humpty Dumpty view of the language. They use, for example, disinterest, fulsome, mitigate and, as a reader pointed out this week, nubile and chauvinist and decimate, to mean what they choose those words to mean. However, as the editor of the Guardian style guide pointed out to the reader who complained about our use of those last three, all of which have changed their meaning or at least relaxed sufficiently to embrace a new and commonly used one, 'There are battles worth fighting, and there are battles that have been lost.'

In the case of disinterest, fulsome and mitigate the battle is by no means lost. These are words which retain specific and useful meanings and which, insofar as it is within my poor capacity to defend them, I shall. My colleague rejected the complaints about nubile and chauvinist and decimate because hardly anyone, he said, used them in the sense that the dictionaries still promote as their primary meaning: ready or suitable for marriage (nubile), aggressive or fanatical patriotism (chauvinism), to kill every 10th man (decimate). He is right, but there is still room for sloppy and incorrect usage: Arsenal decimated the opposition.

A colleague asked me this week whether he could get away with the use of 'gay' in the sense of carefree and merry. Sadly, but wisely, he chose another word. A word cannot easily be stripped of the associations it acquires in common use, although it is not impossible.

This brings me to the increasingly popular word 'heist' which has appeared in both headlines and the text of news stories in the Guardian in the past week, used as a noun to mean robbery: 'Robbers fled with £4.6m in a meticulously planned heist at Heathrow . . .'. It has occurred more than 80 times in the past year: 'Dome heist may have been Met PR stunt, says raider', 'Despite a handful of heists almost all the cash arrived safely', and so on.

The great train robbery has become 'the 1963 heist' or, more indicative, 'the heist of the century'. After I questioned our use of the word, at one of the editor's morning conferences this week, a colleague, defending its use, directed me to the BBC website where there is a list of 'Great heists of our time', including the great train robbery, 'perhaps one of Britain's most notorious heists'. Ah, well.

Collins dictionary, the Guardian's default authority when the style guide provides no help, which is the case here, says: Slang, chiefly US and Canadian: n 1 a robbery; vb 2 (tr) to steal or burgle [variant of hoist].

Eric Partridge in his Dictionary of Slang (eighth edition, 1984) suggests it came into use in Britain, adopted from the US, in about 1965. He concurs with other authorities who think it may be a variant of hoist with a Yiddish origin and he points to the German *er heisst*, he hoists. A 1991 Webster, giving the noun and verb heist (heisted, heisting, and adding heister), describes it as slang gaining currency in the US in the late 1920s as an alternative to hoist – a dockland crane.

I have not found a dictionary that gives the word legitimate status. They all describe it as slang. You can legitimise it yourselves, of course, simply by using it.

It has clearly been boosted by its use in 'movies'. If you tap the word into the Internet Movie Database, about 20 cinema and television movies, led by David Mamet's recent Heist, come up, most of them in the past decade.

My objection to the introduction of the word to the news pages of the paper is only partly based on its history in American slang. It is mainly because it is consciously or unconsciously drawing parallels with crime as portrayed in films, it is inviting us to admire the way in which the crime was planned and the daring of those who carried it out. It is tending to blur fact and fiction.

Sometimes there actually appears to be a symbiosis. In a report in March last year about the capture of a gang of armed robbers, we said, 'The gang's spectacular heists often appeared to come straight out of a Hollywood script.'

I do not think heist should be hijacked by the Guardian's news pages. What do you think?

'That's a great deal to make one word mean,' Alice said in a thoughtful tone.

'When I make a word do a lot of work like that,' said Humpty Dumpty, 'I always pay it extra.'

All word definitions with the aid of Collins dictionary.
Lewis Carroll: Alice's Adventures In Wonderland and
Through The Looking-Glass (Penguin Classics).

Word power: our role in the evolution of language
→ 02 March 2002

Your responses to these Saturday* pieces are always welcome and I am sorry that we do not discuss them more often. A recent column on headlines, which included a reader's comment on the use, the overuse, he argued, of the word 'fury', drew messages of support and protest. They still arrive.

'The lead item in last Wednesday's paper was headlined, "Fury at Byers bail-out . . ." . Nowhere in the article was there anyone who seemed furious – a mildly disgruntled Labour MP, but fury, no. Did you not write about this some time ago?' Indeed I did, but without any comment of my own.

'Fury – violent or uncontrolled anger, wild rage,' is the definition given by Collins. This is rarely what is meant when the word is used in a newspaper. Perhaps on this occasion it was nearer to the truth than is sometimes the case. We have certainly been closer to fury than to mild disgruntlement. But there is no doubt that we are witnessing the degradation of the word, and words once degraded rarely recover.

There is an interesting passage in Boswell's Life of Johnson. Boswell is about to leave Dr Johnson in Harwich: 'I happened to say it would be terrible if he would not find a speedy opportunity of returning to London, and being confined in so dull a place. Johnson: "Don't, Sir, accustom yourself to use big words for little matters. It would not be terrible, though I were to be detained some time here".'

And Boswell comments: 'The practice of using words of disproportionate magnitude is, no doubt, too frequent every where . . .' Let us settle for that.

It is probably a phase we are going through. Nearly 50 years ago it was something else. A reader wrote in 1955: 'There is a gremlin at work among your sub–editors causing them to write headline after headline in bouncing trochaics.' He or she (C Garton of Newcastle-upon-Tyne) then gave – in verse – a selection of the 23 examples discovered in the single issue of the paper of October 19. Here is a flavour: British ships leave Soviet waters /No agreement on joint claim./ Other overseas stock markets?/Underwater traffic jam./ No late drinks for circus artists . . . and so on.

You were equally engaged by a brief survey in the column a couple of weeks ago of the increasing use of the word 'heist' in the Guardian – a word in the process of being not degraded or downgraded but upgraded, against some resistance. I said I did not think it should be used on the news pages of the paper.

Opinion was divided. There were those who agreed: 'It seriously belittles the impact on victims of an armed robbery.' There were others who expressed a certain amount of forlorn sympathy: 'Heist is an ugly word, but not worth going into battle over. The headline writers will win in the end on this one.'

A former colleague wrote, 'I suspect, as you implicitly do, that "heist" is popular both because it has a slightly seedy-glamorous American undertone and it is shorter than robbery/hijack/bank raid etc. Like many another headlineable word, it has passed down into the body of the story and then out into the general word-pool.'

There were one or two readers who saw nothing at all wrong with it. There was more agitation about my attribution to Partridge's Dictionary of Slang, the eighth edition, 1984, of a possible connection to the German '*er heisst*, he hoists'. Er heisst is 'he is called', 'his name is' and the dictionary does not provide any supporting definition of *heissen*. Perhaps, it was suggested, *er hisst*. Partridge does indeed say '*er heisst*', but I notice the entry is, in turn, attributed to RS – Ramsey Spencer, whom Partridge acknowledges for 'copious notes and helpful comments over the years'. Perhaps, one reader suggested, Homer nodded – Homer or one of his helpers.

Another reader objected to my use of the idea of legitimate and illegitimate as a distinction between formal or written speech and colloquial speech or slang. 'Slang,' he said, 'is as "legitimate" as any other form of English.' His authority is Sir James Murray in the 'general explanations' of the first edition of the Oxford English Dictionary.

I shall conclude with a quotation from a wonderful book about Murray (details below). The words, summarising Murray's view, are those of Elisabeth Murray, his granddaughter: '. . . language is a constantly changing, growing thing and cannot be standardised and preserved for ever as it was at any particular point in time by excluding new words because they are considered decadent. . . .' We are participants, though, and therefore not passive. So speak out.

Correction (Published March 5th 2002) attached to this article: In his column, page 7, Saturday Review, March 2, the readers' editor said the dictionary provided no supporting definition for *heissen* – to hoist. In fact, it does. Langenscheidts Handwörterbuch, 6th edition, 1992, includes it, although *hissen* is more common. Several readers had suggested that a reference to this meaning of *heissen* in Partridge's Dictionary of Slang must be incorrect. It is not.

Boswell's Life of Johnson, edited by RW Chapman (Oxford). Caught in the Web of Words: James Murray and the Oxford English Dictionary by KM Elisabeth Murray was reissued in paperback by Yale last year.

*The Open Door Column now appears on Monday.

Mind field: when humour becomes insensitivity
→ 09 March 2002

Earlier this week we published a letter to the editor from a representative of a campaigning group called Mind Out for Mental Health, complaining about an article by a psychiatrist, a junior doctor who writes for the paper under the pen name Michael Foxton.

His columns appear on the health pages of G2, the tabloid second section of the Guardian. They try to do something eminently worthwhile, which is to share with the reader the experience of frontline work in the health service. The doctor addresses his audience in uninhibited language, revealing his own doubts and anxieties with a sometimes scatological humour. One of the useful messages of his columns is: if the patient is human, so is the doctor. The headline on this particular column read: 'The junior doctor is terrified by a large and aggressive psychiatric patient. So where's the panic button?'

Michael Foxton told me that the piece was intended to be about his overreaction and inexperience in dealing with a young man who was being playful and slightly threatening. He said he did not want to lose sight of the fact that aggression and actual violence were not the norm. His column was about what he called 'an in-at-the-deep-end' episode early on in his psychiatric career. He said: 'In medicine, we generally don't hear the mundaner stories of normal, fallible human beings doing their best, or sometimes just doing enough to get by because they're too tired to do their best.'

To return to the published complaint. The writer said, 'Michael Foxton's article . . . served as an urgent reminder of just how much remains to be done to combat stigma and discrimination surrounding mental health. Granted, this tale was intended to be light-hearted and amusing. However, as is often the case, this levity came at the expense of the psychiatric patient depicted, and succeeded in perpetuating the damaging stereotypes of people with mental health problems.

'The man in question, known to have schizophrenia, was portrayed in the usual negative light: menacing, aggressive, posing a serious physical threat to all and sundry. . . . There was talk of panic buttons and alarms, of old ladies being knifed. . . . The only panic buttons and alarm bells that came to mind were those calling for a more responsible and professional representation of mental health in the press.'

This was not the only complaint. There were about half a dozen and, clearly, word had gone round about this particular column. The letters, nevertheless, were individual and heartfelt: 'Could you try and explain to him that making facile jokes about the mentally ill isn't actually funny?'

'Why on earth was it allowed to be published, considering the Guardian's supposed reputation for informed mental health reporting?'

One response came from Professor Arthur Crisp of the Royal College of Psychiatrists, the chairman of the campaign group Changing Minds: Every Family in the Land. He said: 'For those of us concerned to reduce the damaging impact of stigmatisation of people with mental illnesses, Dr Foxton's presentation is troubling. Our own campaign highlights the fact that one in four of us will experience major mental health problems at some stage in our lives, with "every family in the land" involved. Such illnesses are rarely accompanied by aggressive behaviour towards others.

'. . . As a rather junior doctor, he seems to have been ill prepared for the encounter and without consultant cover. As reported, the main faults lie there.'

Professor Crisp added, 'People with mental illness deserve a better press. . . . I am surprised that the Guardian felt obliged to publish such an isolated negative image.'

My sympathies, as you may have deduced, are largely with those complaining. I have made this view clear to Michael Foxton and his editor. As I said to some of those who wrote to me, the Guardian has spent a great deal of effort trying to project the idea of an inclusive society to which the very great many people who have had, or will have, a mental illness belong. It would be odd indeed if a column by a psychiatrist appeared to be working in the opposite direction. In this case, between the intention and the effect, something went wrong.

Lesser evils: the corrections that got away
→ 16 March 2002

A reader writes: 'Could we have your thoughts on what sort of errors are significant and which are not?' Ah, significant. It is a reasonable question. The little blurb at the end of the Guardian's daily corrections column says, 'It is the policy of the Guardian to correct significant errors as soon as possible.'

From November 1997, when the column was introduced, to January 2000, that word was significantly absent. The blurb had simply said, 'It is the policy of the Guardian to correct errors.' This led to a great deal of insistence from one or two readers that the particular error, often something of startling triviality, that they had pointed out should be corrected. After a couple of years I got quite fed up with this and inserted the word 'significant' (important, notable, momentous, as Collins defines it) as a form of self-protection. It has not helped much.

The blurb has never said, 'The Guardian undertakes to correct all errors' – and that is a significant omission. I have written several times in this column to explain that this is because, as the poor child in Jude the Obscure put it, they are too many.

Nor does the blurb say, 'The Guardian does not undertake to overlook insignificant errors.' The first two or perhaps three definitions in Collins apply here: 1) having little or no importance, trifling 2) almost or relatively meaningless 3) small or inadequate. Indeed, errors that fit one or more of these 'insignificant' definitions have, you might almost say, made the corrections column what it is. They have ensured, largely because they are often funny, that the column meets one of Lord Northcliffe's essential requirements for popular – pass over that word quickly – journalism, and is talked about. Thus, when there really is a noise in the corrections column, there is someone there to hear it.

The fact that the column is not confined to 'significant' corrections leads to much correspondence along the following lines, 'If you want to correct "significant errors", as claimed, then this one is at least as important as some of the rather silly homophones that you claim to be significant' (Oh no I don't). The error that this reader was pointing out was the misspelling of the name of the Manchester City footballer, Ali Benarbia, as Ali Bernabia. 'It's an actual error, the misspelling of someone's name. It ought, therefore, to get a correction . . . Are you content to get people's names wrong?'

How dare you, sir. You are speaking to the person who has practically eradicated in the Guardian the misspelling of Lucian Freud. The rogue Lucien, having occurred six times in the year 2000, cropped up only once last year, and so far, only once this year in an item on our website. When people ask me if I have achieved anything in my four years in this job, this is what I proudly hold aloft. And who is it, may I ask, who now stands protectively over Judi Dench, fending off the unwanted Judys? Am I content to get people's names wrong, indeed! And by the way, we did correct Benarbia.

For that matter, how trivial is the homophone? Everyone, even the most literate among you, produces them. If you think you do not, then it must be that you have not noticed. Take this one, describing a walk in the French Alps: 'It was glorious, wading ankle deep, sinking knee deep, thigh deep, waste deep in the loose dry powdery snow.' It is not a misprint. That is what was written by James Murray, the presiding genius of the first great Oxford English Dictionary (from Caught In the Web of Words by KM Elisabeth Murray, Yale).

I had an email last week from a reader who complained that, though he had written frequently, not one of his suggested corrections had appeared. When I checked the email archive, 17 communications from him came up in the past couple of years. I told him what I have frequently said: that the ratio of calls to corrections has remained remarkably consistent at between five and six to one.

This prompted him to remark, 'It sounds like a lottery . . . If it is a lottery, the clear inference to be drawn is that the Guardian is not sticking to its stated corrections policy.' How so?

Significant matters include those in which the personal or professional reputation of an individual or organisation is unjustifiably attacked or damaged; where a factual inaccuracy is so gross that it seriously detracts from the integrity of the story; where reference to race, religion, gender seems to step over the line between free speech and abuse, causing serious offence to a named individual and so on.

They form a small proportion of corrections. Among the vast volume of other things, one does what one can. To quote Edmund Burke, 'No man can make a greater mistake than he who did nothing because he himself could only do a little.'

Taste matters: crossed lines on the Queen Mother and Holy Week

→ 13 April 2002

I returned to work after a break over Easter and the death of the Queen Mother to be greeted with complaints about the Guardian's coverage of both of these events. The newsdesk took the following message – cholerically early – on Wednesday this week: 'I'd just like to complain about the utter hypocrisy shown by your editor in attending the Queen Mother's funeral. . . . Did you know that you are thoroughly despised and detested by the vast majority of this country? You are the scum of the earth.'

'Hypocrisy', presumably because of the paper's declared republican sympathies. Was there no reason to attend the funeral then other than to show unqualified support for the monarchy?

Similar sentiments to those voiced by that caller have been put in letters intended for publication rather than as any formal objection to me. The paper has given ample opportunity for the expression of views on its letters page. Only the smaller part of the mail received by the letters editor has been perceptibly pro-monarchy or critical of the Guardian's coverage. According to the letters editor, the proportion immediately after the Queen Mother's death that might be described as sympathetic was about 10 per cent of the total, rising to 25 per cent or 30 per cent around the time of the funeral. Some fairly sour notes have been sounded during that period.

I did receive more than one complaint from readers who thought the Guardian's republicanism tainted the coverage. 'As a small but futile gesture, I shall stop taking the Guardian during a suitable period of mourning.'

There were perhaps a dozen complaints about the picture of the Queen across seven columns of our front page on the day after the funeral. The headline ran: 'Farewell to a mother, a queen and a symbol of a bygone age.' The picture was used as it was presented to the paper by the photographer who took it, with the image cut off just beneath the Queen's eyes on which attention was therefore focused. Several of you thought this was disrespectful and intrusive. In my view it was neither. Even without the suggestion of the headline it would have provided a thought-provoking and moving image from a memorable event.

The objections about the contents of the Guardian over Easter were directed at two items in particular. One was a column in the Weekend magazine on March 30, in which the writer said, 'In my opinion, the reason why [the Roman Catholic church] is so dead set against abortion is so that its priests can have a ready stream of children to molest . . .' There are no prizes for identifying the writer.

The other was the Diary which had appeared the day before, that is on Good Friday, and was largely concerned with a satire on Christianity and the Crucifixion in particular. One section related a joke, the pay-off of which was Jesus saying, 'I'll tell you what, mother, sometimes you don't half piss me off.' The Diary concluded with a story from a comedian, the late Bill Hicks, which included the line, 'You think when Jesus comes back he ever wants to see a fucking cross again?'

Some readers found all this very excessive and I am inclined to agree with them, even after allowing for the fact that both of the items objected to, the column and the Diary, have clearly announced through past performance their mission to outrage.

One reader raised the familiar complaint that Christians have heaped upon them abuse which those of other faiths would be spared or not expected to tolerate. The timing of the Diary caused particular offence. The joke, the ancient joke as one objector described it, in which Jesus addresses his mother, should not have been used at all according to some. 'The other references would have been tolerable on their own on another day, but not accumulated to insult on a deeply holy day.'

Another wrote, 'On Good Friday of all days of the year, could there [not have been] a moratorium on anti-Christian mockery?' That was from a reader who said she usually enjoyed the diarist's 'pricking of the pompous and hypocritical'. And another, 'Surely a considerable lapse in editorial taste and judgment, particularly in a Good Friday edition?' I think so.

Paradoxically – quixotically was how one person put it – the Diary ran in a column alongside an article by a former religious affairs correspondent of the Guardian on the theme of Good Friday and the meaning of the cross. It was widely, and rightly, praised by readers and quoted in some sermons over Easter. This and another piece on the Resurrection which appeared on the Comment pages on Easter Monday were welcomed almost with disbelief.

Who was it who said the Guardian is a broad church? Sometimes perplexingly so.

Softly, softly: Unlimited freedom of speech – well, almost
→ 20 April 2002

The freest free speech in the Guardian is probably that found on the talk boards of our website. The latter embody one of the primary democratic virtues of the internet, in theory at least: unmediated discourse on any subject with the unrestricted participation of anyone who has anything to say. They began on the Guardian's website almost immediately after its launch a little over three years ago.

The Guardian provides the forum, generically known as 'the Talk', and during a month many thousands of you – in some months perhaps 200,000 or more – take advantage of that. With around four million page impressions – page views – a month, it vies with the jobs as the second most popular site, after news, on Guardian Unlimited.

The subjects most discussed over the past few months have been the Middle East, the aftermath of September 11 and the 'War on Terror', then domestic politics and other domestic issues. These discussions have been conducted by the participants themselves, for the most part in the tones of a civilised, if lively, conversation: we shall come to the departures, lapses and penalties in a minute.

There is no close parallel for this kind of exchange, in its immediacy and degree of freedom, anywhere else in the Guardian, although it might be seen as an expression of a principle that moves the paper as a whole. Restrictions of any kind run counter to its spirit. Those responsible for this area of the website run it with a minimum of rules and with an instinct not to intervene, to edit or delete or censor. The proven principle is that abstinence makes the user grow fonder.

At its best, the talk board epitomises the kind of interactivity – in this case user-to-user – that the paper wants with its readership as a whole. However you define a Guardian reader, passivity is unlikely to be considered a primary characteristic.

Anyone can have access to the talk boards by registering and providing an email address, password and a user name which will sign all that user's contributions to the running debates. This will enable that user to post remarks in any of the discussions taking place, or to start a new one.

Talk board users are an obvious expression of the idea of community on the internet and on Guardian Unlimited in particular (groups of the Guardian's users sometimes arrange to meet in a pub or cafe). When you use the talk boards you show your pass at the door, so to speak, and enter a kind of club in which a huge number of conversations are going on simultaneously. The quality of these conversations, although often high, varies greatly and is sometimes quite poor. Good or bad, all the utterances remain with a frozen spontaneity to be scrutinised later and sometimes objected to.

Everyone who participates in these conversations should be aware of Guardian Unlimited's talk policy. It is as much an appeal as a warning. 'We want the Talk to be the place on the net where you will always find lively, entertaining and, above all, intelligent discussions. The last thing the net needs is yet another site where any attempt at conversation is drowned out by a few people hurling mindless abuse at each other.'

It goes on to say that sometimes, and reluctantly, some postings have to be removed, and indicates the reasons why this might be done. 'We discourage obscenity and mindless abuse. . . . We will not tolerate racism, sexism or homophobia. We will remove any content that may put us in legal jeopardy. . . . We will consider removing any content that other users might find extremely offensive or threatening. If you act with maturity and consideration for other users, you should have no problems on our boards.'

And so we come to the space between theory and practice. More bans are being imposed than at any time since the talk boards started, although we are still speaking of a tiny number. Where it was once extremely rare to ban a user, there are now on average two bannings or banishments a week. Because of the ease with which some email addresses and user names can be changed, however, it is possible that a few individuals are being repeatedly banned under different names.

More postings than before are being removed, and users warned that they risk banning by breaches of the few guidelines. Some have been warned because of racist remarks in the context of the Middle East conflict.

Although vigilance is exercised, it is impossible to watch all the talk boards all the time. Users themselves will usually draw attention to something that seems to abuse and therefore threaten the freedom that they enjoy. The present policy of intervention as rarely as possible is still the correct one and possibly the only one.

Vile bodies: knowing when to stop for decency's sake

→ 27 April 2002

Complaints involving matters of taste, as many of them do, are never very easy to adjudicate. Indeed they are often so difficult – because opinion is so subjective and therefore so variable – that some regulatory bodies will not consider them at all.

Others, as one former regulator told me, try to devise some test for themselves, to draw a dividing line between taste and decency – a difficult and controversial business. It perhaps does no more than recognise, by implication, that there is a scale of what is permissible and what is not – although this changes too. For example, would a picture of a couple copulating, the relevant organs displayed, be tolerated in the pages of the Guardian?

The answer is, apparently, yes. We carried such an image on the arts pages about six months ago, with our review of Ukiyo-e prints at the Royal Academy of Arts. Admittedly the illustration was little bigger than a postage stamp so those who pored over it for long enough to discern the detail might have caught themselves in a censorial caricature and resisted any impulse to complain. How many people actually registered offence? None. Yet, I am pretty sure, nothing like it had been used in the paper before.

The fact is that if it is art, for most of you, the limits of tolerance are greatly extended. I am aware of only one objection to the cover of G2, our tabloid second section, about a month ago when it showed the flayed cadaver of a man from the exhibition, Body Worlds, of work by the German scientist Gunther von Hagens. The question posed, presumably with some confidence, beside the image was: But is it art?

One person, it has been reported, took violent exception to the display of human bodies and parts in this way and attacked one of the exhibits with a hammer. Readers of the Guardian received it more calmly, perhaps partly because by the time the paper used the images they, or very similar ones, were familiar to a great many people through television.

On the day that G2 carried this cover, there appeared on page 12 of the main paper a photograph of daffodils on the shore of Ullswater with a report that a hybrid intruder was threatening to deprive us of the scene, the host of golden daffodils, that Wordsworth saw. This apparently idyllic view was welcomed by a reader who thought that the paper's picture policy had changed in a trend away from this sort of thing towards 'often unpleasant' hard news pictures (he made no mention of the flayed corpses).

'For me, [this tendency] ended a 10-year habit of clipping beautiful photographs and sending them to an Oregon friend. . . . Today's issue offers the first opportunity in three years to use my scissors again. Does this portend a welcome reversion of policy?' I am afraid not.

The reader who complained about the G2 cover picture was also among about a dozen of you who objected to pictures that had appeared in our Weekend magazine a few days earlier, illustrating a feature about a 'colonic irrigation holiday'. The headline – The enema within – was followed by a warning: 'Best not to read this article before breakfast.' One of the pictures showed a young woman holding a colander containing the evacuated material 'sluiced out of her innards', as the caption put it.

This and the flayed corpse were too much: 'These were awful errors of taste, and worse still, totally pointless . . . [beyond] perhaps an infantile desire to shock.' They had driven this reader almost to the point of giving up the paper.

Another awful error of taste, according to some readers, appeared on the front page of the main broadsheet paper on the Saturday of the colonic irrigation feature. This was a deep, four-column close-up portrait of the multiply pierced face of a man participating in a modern primitives exhibition in Germany. One of the dozen readers who complained about this said, 'I work in the theatre and performance studies so am used to seeing examples of body art etc . . . but do not expect to be confronted with it at breakfast where the image could distress others' – he mentioned his two very young children. Another reader wrote, 'To show this deranged self-mutilation on any page of a daily newspaper . . . is disgraceful.' It was indeed a disturbing image and in my view it is doubtful whether its use in colour on the front page was justified.

Opinion in the paper tends to the view that the magazine's poo picture was a mistake – although about 40 readers wrote for more information about the treatment the article described. There is sympathy with anyone offended by the Body Worlds pictures, but a division of opinion on whether publishing them was the right thing to do. Is it a generational thing?

War and pieces: criticism of our Middle East coverage
→ 18 May 2002

This week I circulated Guardian staff, and not just the journalists, with the following questionnaire: Do you think the Guardian's Middle East coverage has been fair or unfair to the Israeli side? Has it been fair or unfair to the Palestinians? Has it been anti-semitic? Has it been anti-Islam (or anti-Palestinian). Do you think the coverage has changed in any way in recent weeks?

General comments were invited and many of the 30 or so who responded chose to give me their views entirely in this form and to ignore the questionnaire so I cannot give you tabulated results. The intention, in any case, was simply to let you in on some of the thinking inside the Guardian. I tried to put the questions in a way that did not suggest a particular response. The majority of those who answered believe the coverage has been good and generally fair.

First, here are the views of a non-journalist colleague who believes it has been unfair to the Israeli side, anti-semitic and indulgent to the Palestinians: 'I am sure I will be the lone voice in criticising [the] treatment of the conflict, but without exception my friends (and not all of them are supportive of Sharon) feel the paper is virulently anti-Israel (and anti-semitic) and not one of them would consider buying it. My own family were loyal Guardian readers but stopped in the 1990s because of its relentless hostility towards Israel . . . [Now I] try very hard not to read articles about the conflict as they only succeed in disappointing me with their blatant anti-Israel sentiments and the plain inaccuracy of the reporting.'

She lists examples, with Jenin at the head. 'I was utterly disgusted at the front page headline "Massacre" regarding Jenin. The newspaper has a responsibility, especially given how delicate the situation is, not to report such damaging accusations unless it has the proof to back it up. Where was the bold headline saying, "Lies, there was no massacre"?' [The Guardian carried a review of press coverage of Jenin, Media, May 6, by the London correspondent of the Israeli newspaper Ha'aretz.]

The comments I have quoted strongly reflect complaints from Jewish, or pro-Israeli readers, which far outweigh complaints from pro-Palestinian or other sources.

In fact the Guardian has not at any time applied the word 'massacre' to the events at Jenin. On Wednesday April 17, it carried the following headline across the front page: Israel faces rage over 'massacre'. The word was enclosed in single quotation marks – a subtlety lost in the passions generated. The accompanying report, beneath the bylines of three staff journalists, recorded the Commons debate in which Gerald Kaufman denounced Mr Sharon as a 'war criminal'. It did not attribute the term 'massacre' to Mr Kaufman. It made it clear that it came from a leading Palestinian, Nabil Shaath. It also quoted an Israeli government spokesman dismissing the allegations as 'ridiculous'.

The sensitivity is easily understood. But it cannot be said too often that the coverage should be judged over a period. A senior correspondent and commentator, who believes the coverage in general has been 'pretty good and pretty balanced', felt that the paper's overall reporting of Jenin showed its skill in getting the facts and 'getting them from both sides'. A piece featuring Palestinian anger and distress should be seen against a contrasting report 'about Israel soldiers' anger that the restraint they showed in the Jenin operation was not recognised'. He believes the Guardian made it clear from the start that 'there was no real likelihood of a Jenin massacre and kept the larger picture in view better than other journals'.

He made this point, however, about balance. 'It does not mean what some insist on, namely that every time Sharon is criticised there must be a sideswipe at Arafat, or that every time Israeli operations are mentioned, the most recent suicide bombings must be recalled in considerable detail.

'Balance does not mean that blame must be equally apportioned – much of the American coverage that is, up to a point, critical of Israel suffers from this false symmetry . . . We do not normally fall into the trap of this deeply unbalanced balance.'

One colleague, not involved in the Middle East coverage said, 'I am fed up with being reproached every time I tell any active member of the Jewish community that I work for the Guardian.' He did feel there was cause for concern. He felt, for instance, that – to revert to Jenin – the use of the word 'massacre', even in inverted commas, was 'extremely prejudicial. . . . A day later we were writing that there was no evidence of a massacre at all.'

I shall continue this next week, with more comments and the views of the editor and foreign editor.

Balancing act: charges that the paper has been anti-semitic

→ 25 May 2002

Many of the Guardian journalists who responded to my invitation to give their views on the paper's coverage of the Israeli-Palestinian conflict commented on accusations, levelled in correspondence from Jewish readers, that it has been anti-semitic.

One or two thought there had been occasional lapses which might have encouraged an inclination to see it that way – a reference to 'the comparative wealth and position of Britain's Jewish community', was one phrase cited and compared with a piece which referred to Jewish control of Hollywood and the media. (The latter was 18 months ago and I responded to it then by saying it contained statements which were understandably construed as anti-semitic.) Another journalist, citing similar examples, thought that a few months ago the coverage was 'so anti-Israeli it was embarrassing'.

There was a strong rejection by practically everyone of the suggestion that the coverage was permeated by anti-semitism, an impression that sometimes appears to have been formed remotely: 'My Jewish family think we only publish pro-Palestinian pieces and opinions because that's what they read in the Jewish press.' Many read only selected articles circulated to them by lobbies.

One of the paper's leading commentators believes the perception of anti-semitism among the Jewish readership derives more from tone and a sense that the Guardian sees humanity only on the Palestinian side, that it will explain Palestinian action in a way less readily afforded to the Israelis. Jewish readers, he said, 'are telling us loud and clear an inconvenient truth: that they see Israel as a version of themselves, that an attack on the Jewish state is an attack on Jews, whether we like it or not.

'The Guardian is a progressive paper with a noble history: we were first in the British press to realise the persecution of the Jews in Nazi Germany and we were an early backer of the Zionist project. But now we are seen as a paper that is hostile to the Jews, one even liberal Jews cannot read any more.'

One journalist insisted: It is not anti-semitic to criticise the brutal and racist regime of Ariel Sharon . . . it is not anti-semitic to hear the voices of the Palestinians, it is not anti-semitic to see Palestinians as the victims of a situation in which they are overwhelmingly the underdog.'

A senior Guardian journalist said: 'One of the biggest problems for reporters [has been] to withstand the – clearly orchestrated – pressure to equate any criticism of Israeli government action with anti-semitism.

. . . The blackmail of making one feel ashamed to criticise Israeli actions . . . [can lead] to immeasurable damage.'

A running criticism of the range of comment in the Guardian was, in fact, that it was short of articulate Palestinian and Muslim voices, some of which among the latter would be critical of the Palestinians.

The foreign editor believes that throughout the Guardian far more space has been devoted to the conflict than in other newspapers – some think too much, at the expense of other parts of the world whose problems seem devalued by disproportion. He thinks this may be partly because of the Guardian's role mentioned earlier.

'We were part of Israel's foundation and it is a part of our history. . . . The problem for our Jewish readers is that this time round we are perceived as not supporting Israel. That is a misconception. We support Israel but we do not support this government . . . we are committed to telling the story, to showing the terror caused by suicide bombing but also to showing the oppression – I think that is the correct word – of the Palestinians. We will not be browbeaten into being bland.'

The editor of the Guardian says: 'The situation is very grave, very violent on both sides and the difficulties of reporting it are horrendous – your reporter being shot at by Israeli forces on the ground.

'The Israelis' information network and monitoring of the press is much more active and professional than the Palestinians'. We have a role in articulating their case – giving a voice to the voiceless is how I put it – but not disproportionately or uncritically.

'Our leader line has been very critical of the Sharon government which is, in our view, in a cul-de-sac. We think that to identify Israel with Bush's war on terrorism is a grossly simplified reading of the situation. We have also said that Arafat is a busted flush and criticised the surrounding Arab nations for their failure to play any constructive role. But, in the end, we think friends of Israel should not shy away from criticising the behaviour of a government which, in our view, is harming the cause of Israel itself.'

The right to be heard: truth and propaganda in the Middle East
→ 03 June 2002

Towards the end of my second article on attitudes to the paper's coverage of the Middle East among its own journalists and other staff, I quoted the editor. He said, in part: 'The Israelis' information network and monitoring of the press is much more active and professional than the Palestinians'. We have a role in articulating their cause – giving a voice to the voiceless . . . but not disproportionately or uncritically.'

The truth of the first part of the statement was quickly borne out by the intervention of the pro-Israeli electronic lobby HonestReporting.com. I had noted that I would be devoting this column to readers' responses. As I write I have had more than 500 emails. I would say that 400 or so came from members of HonestReporting in Israel and in the Jewish diaspora, principally – about 75 per cent of them – from the US.

They had all been circulated with my two articles and some introductory notes that began, 'The Guardian (UK), a frequent target of criticism from HonestReporting has now been forced to take an introspective look at the criticism levelled at them [sic].' It then went on to say that I had 'interviewed the entire Guardian staff . . . [and that] the responses were surprisingly critical'.

The case is different. No one coerced anyone. I gave people working for the Guardian – not just journalists – the opportunity to comment and about 30 people responded (as I said in the first article), a small and perhaps disappointing number when you consider that the paper has more than 350 staff journalists alone.

It was clear that many of the 'readers' who responded had never seen the Guardian at all. Some read it online but others saw only circulated articles – several correspondents told me as much. By the middle of the week, pro-Palestinian groups had become aware of the HonestReporting lobby and this was reflected in a rise in the number of emails begging the Guardian not to give in to it but to continue to give the Palestinians a voice in the debate.

I have, in fact, read all the emails. I have replied, usually briefly, to about half of my correspondents. All the emails, including my replies, sit in a queue that is permanently available to all Guardian editorial staff at their desks. The arguments voiced will have the widest possible circulation within the Guardian.

I have read it all, from all sources, because that way I can see that all the emails are individual and strongly felt, and the abusive emails are a tiny minority. These are among the ones that I have tried to reply to – usually with a question: how do you see the conflict being resolved? How do you see that happening if we do not talk to each other? How can we talk sensibly, if we turn a deaf ear to one side or the other?

Readers of the paper will have noted that last week two extraordinary events took place in Britain, both sponsored by the Guardian: one, in London, was a debate between Yasser Abed Rabbo, a member of Yasser Arafat's cabinet, and Yossi Beilin, the former Israeli justice minister (which could not have taken place in Israel because of current restrictions). The other, outside London, was the Guardian Middle East dialogue, a conference between representatives of the Israelis and Palestinians and politicians from Northern Ireland.

I have no doubt that the perception of the Guardian as anti-semitic is genuine among those who hold it. I hope the arguments and the anxieties behind them, and the complaints about individual pieces, will continue to be heard and examined. In particular, I hope the fears expressed by many of you that ill-considered or highly emotive language may contribute to an atmosphere at large in which anti-semitism could flourish are taken seriously, as they deserve to be.

I do not think the Guardian is anti-semitic. Many Jewish readers here in Britain agree with me. 'Without doubt the Guardian's coverage is far more balanced and closer to the truth then any other publication in this country. . . . As a Jew who cares for the survival of my own tradition I hope you will continue to maintain and develop this course of action.' But here is the view of another Jewish correspondent in Britain: 'Almost all members of the UK Jewish community hold your paper and its ilk responsible for the re-emergence of anti-semitic acts in this country on a scale last seen in the 30s . . .'.

The process of communication is always flawed. Here it is doubly difficult because of the propaganda war that is distorting the discourse. But I think the Guardian is right to maintain open access to the platform. As an Edinburgh reader put it: 'We must have the opportunity to hear both sides of the conflict for there to be a just peace.'

Memory with a purpose: a welcoming hand from the Scott Trust

→ 17 June 2002

The opening of the Guardian and Observer archive, education and visitor centre – we call it the Newsroom – today marks a significant development in the relationship of both newspapers with their readers. It is housed at 60 Farringdon Road, opposite the main Guardian building in London, in an elegant 19th-century warehouse that has been beautifully and practically turned to its new purpose behind the original facade.

Appropriately, visitors are greeted by Epstein's bust of the Guardian's most famous editor, CP Scott, who appears to stand ready to scrutinise the credentials of the paper's present journalists. Its transfer from the Guardian's original home in Manchester, where it had not been seen by the general public, itself seems to mark a symbolic moment. Those who feel the wrench may console themselves that he guards the entrance to a permanent exhibition in which the history and heritage of both newspapers are concisely displayed.

The Newsroom is entirely an enterprise of the Scott Trust, which now owns both newspapers, developed from a seed planted by the present editor of the Guardian. He had the idea, as I pointed out in a column about a year ago, when on clearing out the office of his predecessor as deputy editor, not long before he himself became editor, he discovered a copy of the first edition of the Manchester Guardian, May 5 1821. It had been perilously close to being discarded. Now it is part of an archive that will preserve documents and photographs under the best possible conditions. It will eventually contain the entire archive of the Observer photographer Jane Bown, and others, and the documentary riflings or savings of recent generations of journalists – some personal confessions and donations in my next column. Some documents and photographs, as visitors from today will discover, are already on view and they will be part of a changing exhibition, a mulling over of the past of the two papers.

The vital role of the Scott Trust will, one hopes, become apparent. The editor believes that the Trust standing in place of a conventional owner – ensuring, I would say, that no editor has had to contend with a ranting baron on the roof – has concentrated the paper's energy on its relationship with its readers. As he puts it, the Guardian has had no other kind of relationship to worry about. The development of the website and access to each other through email has extended and in many ways strengthened the bond (although as we all now know, not without problems).

The Newsroom provides the missing dimensions, the links to the past and the future. The past is obviously important. The loss of memory flattens journalism. It strips away identity. The archive should help to mitigate those effects. Its presence should stay the destructive hand and reduce the alarming loss of cells.

The future will be streaming through the building in the form of groups of young people visiting its schoolroom. It is hoped there will be daily school visits by the autumn. There are two staff education officers and the exhibition and teaching areas are accessible to wheelchair users.

Students (up to 30 in a group) will use state-of-the-art computers and other equipment to explore themes related to their curriculum and often fed by our archive. They will have the opportunity to produce their own newspapers – some who have been in for a trial run have already done that, choosing real stories and pictures, laying out their pages on screen and writing their own headlines (more than one or two have caught our infectious weakness for alliteration).

For young people and adults there are many interactive elements in the exhibition area. You can hear former Guardian journalists, including the paper's last cotton correspondent, describe their experiences. You can listen to the foreign editor describe the way in which the paper reacted to the events and aftermath of September 11. You can select on screen from a variety of pictures and compare your choice with that actually chosen by the Guardian for use on the day.

Very shortly you will be able to test your judgment on ethical issues on which the journalist had to make more or less instant decisions. It might encourage a slightly more sympathetic understanding of aberrations. It should encourage criticism that is better informed and to the point.

I hope it will soon be possible to arrange reader events with an opportunity to meet and question Guardian journalists. There is a lecture theatre with seating for about 90. Meanwhile drop in on weekdays. It is free. Details: guardian.co.uk/newsroom or telephone 020 7886 9898. It is, as you often tell me, your paper.

All our yesterdays and yours too: some of the treasures flowing into the new Newsroom archive

→ 24 June 2002

A perusal of the relatively few documents already displayed in the Newsroom, the Guardian and Observer's new archive and visitor centre in Farringdon Road, London, will indicate the riches to be tapped. There is a letter from George Orwell to David Astor, the editor of the Observer, the notebook kept by Vita Sackville-West for the gardening column she contributed to the Observer when she was creating the gardens at Sissinghurst, and later the notes made by Richard Fry, the Guardian's financial editor (note the versatility), of an interview with Charlie Chaplin, and a letter from Harold Wilson in 1937, apologising for having to decline a job on the Guardian . . .

The pièce de résistance is perhaps a note, in French, provided by Samuel Beckett, introducing the Guardian correspondent in Paris to his agent who was handling invitations to Beckett's film (called Film): 'Dear Jerome [Linden], If you show the film, please be kind and invite my friend Peter Lennon – in spite of his being a journalist. Sam.'

This is just one of a number of billets that were arrested as they passed between Lennon and Beckett. Now that we have an archive there is less justification for hoarding. We shall hand over what we have 'saved' or 'rifled' – in spite of our being journalists. We have an amnesty.

The editor of the Guardian, Alan Rusbridger – setting an example – has recently parted with several boxes of papers accumulated in his own ascent, including notes from Graham Greene and a letter from Diana: other past and present staff members, he hopes, will follow the flow.

There have been some extraordinary gifts. Richard Scott has donated a copy of The World Crisis 1911-1914, sent to his grandfather at the Manchester Guardian in 1923, with the following note from the author: 'My dear [CP] Scott, You were a good friend in the hard days with which this book deals & I hope you will like to have a copy in yr library. Yours sincerely, Winston Churchill.'

Another member of the Scott family, Jessica Scott (the widow of CP Scott's grandson, Laurence Scott), has given a copy of Malcolm Muggeridge's book, Picture Palace (1934), a roman à clef about life in the Manchester Guardian – a rare copy of a book withdrawn when the Guardian's lawyers intervened. It is annotated by John Scott (son of CP), giving the identity of the characters.

The book opens with this passage, with a pencil note 'C.P.S[cott]': 'Old Savoury sat in his room in the offices of the Accringthorpe Courier reading press cuttings about himself . . .. He had sat in this room each evening for fifty years, with printing presses pounding away like a heart beneath him.'

At a party to launch the Newsroom, Geoffrey Taylor, the Guardian historian and former foreign leader writer, surrendered a carved wooden letter opener inscribed to CP Scott 'Token of Appreciation from Boer Prisoners of War. Diyatalawa [Camp], Ceylon. 1902' – the Guardian had spoken out for the proper treatment of Boer prisoners dispersed in camps around the world.

I am handing over my letters: about a dozen from RK Narayan including the typescript of his Tale of a Tub, a reflection on mortality that I persuaded him to write after he had spent hours as a shivering prisoner – a small, soapy and slithering one – in a huge bath at the Dolphin apartments in London (still shaken when I met him the following day), a letter to me and short piece by Satyajit Ray (which his biographer told me may have been the last thing he wrote in English), describing meetings with Rabindranath Tagore. It begins: 'My first acquaintance with Tagore was through his songs. When I was a very small child, my mother used to put me to sleep by singing Tagore songs. Some of them became my favourites and I would ask for them by name when I learned to speak . . .'

I find a lot of other notes and letters have accrued, several, enclosing poems which the Guardian published, from Harold Pinter, others from Chinua Achebe, Ivan Klima, David Grossman (in 1991, declining an invitation because of other work, to write a long essay on his nationality), a letter, an obituary really, in tiny handwriting in lines shortening down the page almost to a point, from John Gielgud, in tribute to his lifelong friend Margaret Harris ('Percy'), one third of the stage-designing team of Motley. And very much more, but paling, I hope, beside the yet uncatalogued archive of the Observer literary editor (and translator of Proust), Terence Kilmartin, who would appreciate the time regained.

Some of my best friends: justified cries of foul from the field of play

→ 01 July 2002

Beware of the horns of a bull, of the heels of a horse, of the smile of an Englishman. – Irish proverb

Many of you write to me in a state of perplexity at the generalised insults offered now and again through the pages of the Guardian at whole groups or – stimulated recently by the World Cup – entire nations.

On Friday last week one Guardian columnist discussed the proposition that, in the words of the heading 'anti-German feeling seems to be the last acceptable prejudice'. It seems reasonable to ask whether all his colleagues share his conclusion that 'no prejudice is acceptable'. He went on: 'Open the door to one form of xenophobia and you will soon find yourself well and truly swamped.'

This is the kind of thing my correspondents expect from the Guardian – a call to reason and reasonableness when the mob is roused. However I do not have to dig far into my postbag to find complaints directed at the Guardian for publishing the kind of stereotypical remarks about the Germans that the article was discussing. Exercises of this kind should, perhaps, be viewed with a degree of scepticism.

The bewilderment of some of you is expressed in terms similar to the following, which comes from a reader complaining about what he saw as a recent unfair attack on the Irish in the context of the World Cup: 'Why is [the columnist] allowed to vent his petulant jealousies in a supposedly "liberal" newspaper which just a few days ago was urging us all to get over our "tribalism"?'

This particular column prompted more than 100 complaints. It had the distinction of rousing a previously unknown (to me that is) Irish lobby which accounted for a proportion of the mail. When I took the complaints to the relevant section editor, he plucked handfuls of hair from his head, complained that the whole thing had been misconstrued and that we were experiencing a (partly) orchestrated humour lapse.

Exactly what did the columnist say that aroused such ire? In the course of a quite short piece headed 'Cheer the Irish? Never', he registered his dismay at the result of the Ireland-Saudi Arabia game. 'I was cheering for the Saudis, out of a respect for their criminal justice system. Given a choice between two right-of-centre agrarian theocracies, I'll go with the more rigorous one, if that's OK.' By the time the column appeared, Ireland had been knocked out by Spain: 'Who will the world cheer for now that the lovable leprechauns have been returned to their misty hills and treacherous bogs?'

One reader wrote: 'I was surprised that your paper, which I believed to be enlightened, would carry such a piece of hatred. Nice to see that the English tradition of fair play and tolerance lives on. I believe in freedom of speech, but . . .. Imagine the shoe being on the other foot.'

A reader from Dublin enquired whether the columnist knew the Guardian was widely available in Ireland. 'I myself wander down my own little misty hill and traverse a particularly treacherous bog every morning to get my copy, although in future I'll be binning any supplement containing that patronising git's column.'

That is enough to give a flavour of the more moderate responses. The columnist is dismayed that what he thought was humorous hyperbole or irony aimed at stereotyping should apparently go so wide of the mark. 'Does anyone really think that I believe the Saudi and Irish regimes are similar?'

The features editor defends the column. The target, he says, was not the Irish but the international and implicitly patronising love affair with the Irish football team – the cliched view of the Irish promoted by their part-time international fan club.

Clearly then, this intention passed by a fairly large number of readers. Several of you suggested that similar remarks would not be allowed about, say, black or Jewish people. The editor of the paper believes that considerable care should be taken not to offend people who have recently been or are at present the objects of discrimination.

You may ask whether that goes far enough. I do not think too much should be made of the case I have been discussing. It is a yellow card, not a red one. But does it represent a tendency?

I have pointed out before that the Press Complaints Commission protects individuals and not groups, arguing for reasonable freedom of speech. It throws responsibility back on the individual journalist. Is it in safe hands?

The epigraph comes from Racial Proverbs edited by Selwyn Gurney Champion, Routledge, 1938.

The need for straight talking: your right to know where we get our information
→ 08 July 2002

Some long-established practices in journalism run contrary to the idea of openness and accountability that the Guardian is trying to pursue. One of these is taking material from other publications and running it or incorporating it, often little altered, with no attribution.

The practice is something which it is perhaps fanciful to think of eradicating completely from the fiercely competitive British press. One of my old papers, the Northampton Mercury – founded 1720 – once had a reputation across the north of England for its comprehensive news coverage. A horse rider carried copies of the London newspapers to Northampton ahead of the main delivery coach. The plums were picked and transferred to the waiting columns of the Mercury and the paper was printed in time to catch the coach for distribution, with the other already rifled papers, further north.

A degree of this still goes on, usually in the hours of night when newsdesks have seen the early editions of their rivals. I was reminded of this a few days ago when I went to the person whose byline appeared on a report to put a query raised by a reader about some figures quoted in it. 'I can't help you there. Those figures were not in the piece I filed. They were written in by the desk.' In fact, they had been taken from the early edition of another newspaper but mistranscribed, making the correction, for the few who knew, perhaps a bit more embarrassing than usual.

Another journalist told me he had recently quoted a senior military figure, attributing his remarks to a published source, but this was struck out on the grounds of space and unwarranted puffery for the general's organisation. This left the impression that the journalist had spoken directly to the general, which he had not. This cannot be right, can it?

Not all that long ago, in a story requiring great sensitivity, we carried long quotations from another person to whom the journalist had not spoken directly. The presentation, withholding from readers the source of the substantial quotations – again another newspaper – left the clear impression that the person had spoken to the Guardian.

I'll quote again from a column of mine about plagiarism (July 1, 2000) in which I referred to a useful American publication, Media Law by Ralph L Holsinger (second edition, McGraw-Hill), where he says: 'Every reporter borrows from the work of other reporters. Reporters working on newspapers in areas served by more than one paper are asked by their editors to follow up stories clipped from competing publications. . . . It's part of the game, and as long as a reporter doesn't take too much, too often, all is well.'

Some discretion is allowed but it is often exercised against the interests of the reader, whose right to know where the stuff is coming from we are supposed to recognise. The substantial unattributed quotations in the last example clearly should have been attributed to their source. The failure to do that brought the following sharp memo from the editor of the Guardian:

'It transpired that the quotes had been lifted from a local newspaper and repeated with no indication that the person concerned had not been speaking to the Guardian.

'This is completely unacceptable. At the very minimum it raises questions of plagiarism. Much more concerning is the issue of trust. If a reader reads something in direct quotation marks in the Guardian he or she is entitled to believe that the reporter can vouch for the accuracy of the quote.

'Copying quotes out of other newspapers without any form of attribution is simply bad journalism, never mind legally risky. If . . . you are going to repeat quotes then always say where they came from. It won't be much help in a legal action, but at least the reader can evaluate the reliability of the source.'

The editor was repeating, in other words, what is said in the Guardian's editorial code under the heading of Plagiarism: 'Staff must not reproduce other people's material without attribution. The source of published material obtained from another organisation should be acknowledged including quotes taken from other newspaper sources . . .'

These editorial guidelines, although quite young, were published – on our website too – before any of the examples I have cited occurred. As I said at the beginning we are, in a way, fighting the habits of more than a lifetime. The editorial code is meant to exert pressure in favour of the reader. The decisions that are taken in the circumstances I have described are easier and more likely to be right when the relationship with the reader is kept in mind.

Revival time: a show of monumental support for Hazlitt
→ 05 May 2001

As a change from the miserable catalogue of complaint (I resist the temptation to say catalogue of miserable complaints) here is something positive. A couple of weeks ago the Saturday Review, the part of the Guardian in which this column appears,* published as its front feature an article by the philosopher AC Grayling about William Hazlitt, described reasonably enough in a headline as 'one of England's greatest writers and radicals'. The aim of the piece was to draw attention to the fact that Hazlitt's grave in St Anne's churchyard in Soho, London, was too modest for someone of his stature, modest almost to the point of anonymity, and to suggest that something more suitable should be placed there.

The way in which readers of the paper have responded to this has been quite astonishing. Numbers are not necessarily an indication of the seriousness of a complaint, but when the paper does something fairly appalling 20 to 30 of you may register a protest.

But letters or calls in support or praise of something? In the two weeks since Grayling's article appeared more than 200 of you have written to say how much you enjoyed reading it, or how moved you were by it (to tears in at least one case) and to contribute, between you, at the time of writing, more than £4,000 towards the cost of the new monument – which may, in fact, be in the region of £20,000.†

I declare an interest. Two or three months ago when I had just finished reading Grayling's recent biography of Hazlitt, The Quarrel of the Age: The Life and Times of William Hazlitt (Weidenfeld and Nicolson), I went to St Anne's churchyard, off Wardour Street, very close to Leicester Square, to look for the grave. I failed to find it but discovered it on a second visit. It lies flat in the grass on the left hand side of the little park that the churchyard now forms.

I asked to be introduced to Grayling and suggested that we should try to restore to the grave a stone bearing the long inscription that was once there but which has totally disappeared. That anything at all there survived the bombing in the second world war is remarkable.

The committee which quickly accrued, and which is driven, I think we could say, by AC Grayling, now includes Michael Foot, Andrew Motion, Tom Paulin, Duncan Wu, Tim Miller of St Anne's, Annalena McAfee, the editor of the Guardian's Saturday Review, and me. The committee has commissioned Lida Kindersley of the Cardozo Kindersley Workshop in Cambridge to design and cut the stone. One reader commented: 'I am absolutely delighted to learn that the Kindersley workshop is handling the commission. The result is bound to be as good as you can get.' The committee has had a warmly encouraging letter of support from the Soho Society.

Everyone has been bowled over by the impetus given to the whole thing by readers of the Guardian. We hope to acknowledge individual contributions in the near future with a letter that Michael Foot will sign on our behalf.

Many of you sent contributions in memory of a parent or grand-parent. I quote from one of your letters: 'My father (a Lancashire cotton weaver) introduced me to Hazlitt's writings during the 1930s when I was about 12 years old. I found them difficult but persevered. My father had a 1910 copy of Lectures on the English Poets and Spirit of the Age and it's now in my possession. I dip into it regularly. What continues to amaze me is how a man, who left school at 12 in 1900, with virtually no education could have a penchant for Hazlitt. It proved to be my gain.'

Several contributions came from places with Hazlitt connections: Maidstone, where he was born, and Hackney, where he attended New College, the dissenting academy. One reader in Maidstone wrote, 'I became interested in his work on receiving a copy of his collected essays as a school prize way back in 1927. I still read them occasionally.' Another came from a minister who preaches sometimes in the Unitarian chapel where Hazlitt's father preached.

One reader wrote: 'I got out my book of Table Talk and started reading it again. I first read Table Talk when 19, aboard a merchant ship in the early 1950s. I loved the book and [it] made a great impression on me, especially On Living to One's Self.'

We shall keep you informed about the progress of the project and certainly aim to let all subscribers know in advance about the unveiling ceremony, which now seems a little nearer. Meanwhile, thank you so much.

* The column now appears on the comment pages on Monday

† About 500 people have now (October 2002) subscribed roughly £18,000 towards a total cost of around £23,000. Lord Bragg (Melvyn Bragg) has become the ninth member of the committee. It is planned to 'unveil' the restored grave on the anniversary of Hazlitt's birthday, April 10, 2003.

Write answers: homophones that test my patience and your wits

→ 23 December 2000

The following note appears in James Thurber's account of his years at the New Yorker under its founding editor Harold Ross. 'A suggestion from a reader: "I have an idea for a cartoon. The cartoon is entitled Pouring over his Books. This is a pun. Have a student sit by a desk with a stack of books before him and reading out of one book. The student is pouring himself a gin and surrounded by a litter of empty bottles. The humour in this cartoon is in the words pour and poir, one means to drink and the other means to study carefully." In the margin of this wondrous note,' Thurber tells us, 'Ross had written "Too subtle"'.

The homophone – a status which 'pour' and the Runyonesque 'poir' almost achieve – stalks the pages of the Guardian, as readers of the daily corrections column might testify. It is 'one of a group of words', these regular readers will not need to be told, 'pronounced in the same way but differing in meaning or spelling or both' (Collins).

I admit to using the word to cover things which are not really homophones but near-homophones and near-misses for the word the writer failed to find in a desultory search that was abandoned too quickly. I would be perfectly happy to admit to failure in reducing the occurrence of homophones in the pages of the Guardian, but the admission would imply that I had expected success. I try to cling to reason. They are an infestation, breeding faster than they can be controlled.

Thurber, had he lived to read the Guardian of today, might have been particularly tickled to learn that 'US polling officials have poured over thousands of ballot papers trying to detect voter intention. 'Pored' was the word that eluded the writer. But this sort of thing, repeated and repeated, would have driven Harold Ross bananas. He, Thurber tells us, 'lived always in the wistful hope of getting out a magazine each week without a single mistake . . . overchecking was better than underchecking . . .'.

Which leads us, nicely, to the readers' editor's homophone test. Give yourself one point for marking the wrong word, and another for identifying the correct one. Maximum score 40 points. Anything over 35: good by our standards.

1 'The proud Danes, [are] used to seeing hoards of Swedes make the 45-minute ferry crossing.'

2 Questions 'that illicit particularly spirited replies'.

3 In a review of the band Radiohead we mentioned '...guitar effects peddles that do everything short of telling jokes... '

4 '... the madly rivalrous dictionaries which destroy the piece of my home'.

5 'Numerical targets become straightjackets for the very people who daily must cope.'

6 The local weather of Hampstead [hill] 'creates its own private and, one might say, rather well-healed cumulus'.

7 'Mr James is unlikely to be phased by the criticisms...'.

8 'The committee considered the use of soldiers to compliment police forces currently marshalling the largely peaceful protests.'

9 '... his gangly build leant itself to professional basketball...'.

10 'She had to reign in some of the college's wilder entrepreneurial activity...'.

11 From the obituary of a film director in which we said one of his characters '... wakes up from sexual ecstasy surrounded by bones and sculls'.

12 In a column we compared the experience of making love with 'being wrapped lightly across the knuckles with a damp envelope.'

13 'The website revolves around a newspaper article detailing the grizzly murder of a character in the film.'

14 A headline: 'China accused of India breech'.

15 In a report about the Ebola virus, we said that local people had been advised 'to suspend cultural practices, such as burial rights'.

16 'In Glaxo's case it was further problems with its controversial treatment for irritable bowl syndrome ...'.

17 From a diary of the floods: 'Started car to venture out for provisions... brakes have ceased, won't move.'

18 'BT, which is expected to formerly announce Brightstar as early as next month...'.

19 In our collected recollections of the day Margaret Thatcher resigned, we quoted someone saying (improbably), 'They had a televised censor motion in the House of Commons and we were glued to it in the office.'

20 From a Country Diary: 'Later I counted 56 whooper swans, including five signets.'

Happy Christmas.

Answers: 1 hordes **2** elicit **3** pedals **4** peace **5** straitjackets (although some dictionaries allow straightjackets) **6** well-heeled **7** fazed **8** complement **9** lent **10** rein in **11** skulls **12** rapped **13** grisly **14** breach **15** rites (but burial rights are not unimaginable) **16** bowel **17** seized **18** formally **19** censure **20** cygnets.

The Thurber story was pointed out by HI Scopes (thanks very much)
and comes from The Years with Ross by James Thurber,
first published in Britain by Hamish Hamilton in 1959.

→ (more) ~~COR~~

~~REC-~~

~~TIONS~~&

→~~Clarific~~

~~-ations~~

Corrections & Clarifications

~~two~~

Corrections
July 2000 → July 2002

→ 09 August 2000

One more hyphen perhaps in the following, from our report about the day it rained sprats in Great Yarmouth, page 2, August 7: 'The two inch-long sprats covered a garden shed and several lawns in the area ...'

→ 10 August 2000

A story yesterday on page 7 named Britain's consul general in Sudan, Lawrence Pickup, as the official who devised a controversial visa form (since withdrawn) designed to prevent asylum seekers reaching Britain. The Foreign Office says Mr Pickup was not the man responsible. It is not quite sure who was.

→ 12 August 2000

A story about a new, cheaper Aston Martin, the DB7, was accompanied in early editions yesterday, page 23, Finance, by a photograph of a Bentley.

In assessing Steven Berkoff's new play, Messiah, an article on page 14, G2, August 10 equated the immaculate conception and Mary's impregnation. This is a recurring misconception, annually corrected in this column. The immaculate conception has nothing directly to do with the birth of Jesus. It is the doctrine that Mary herself was conceived by her mother (St Anne) without the stain of Original Sin. The Virgin Birth is the doctrine of Christ's birth without a human father.

→ 14 August 2000

An article on the TV programme Big Brother wrongly described Nick Bateman as 'a badly dressed stockbroker', after earlier stating, pages 4–5, G2, August 11, that he worked for Lloyd's, which is the insurance market.

→ 21 August 2000

A roundup on the outbreak of swine fever, page 4, the Editor, August 18, said the EU had banned live exports of British pigs. The ban is on pigs from England.

In an article about efforts to get endangered academics out of Nazi Germany and into Britain (Saturday Review, Page 3, August 12) Tess Simpson, 'a young law graduate', was mentioned as the person who became lifelong secretary of the Academic Assistance Council. Actually, her degree was in modern languages (French, German).

→ 23 August 2000

The Roman emperor Claudius could not have patronised the Colosseum (Passnotes yesterday, G2, page 3), as he died in 54AD, roughly two decades before it was built under the emperor Titus Flavius Vespasianus, rendered Vespasian in English. The Byron quotation given ('When falls the Coliseum, Rome shall fall/ And when Rome falls – the world') should have been assigned to Childe Harold's Pilgrimage.

→ 24 August 2000

A heading for Inside Story, G2, page 4, yesterday referred to 'Hollywood's only publically acknowledged lesbian couple'. The word is publicly. In the same edition's broadsheet, page 2, two-minute Guardian flagged our inquiry into 'boardroom renumeration'. Remuneration, that is.

→ 25 August 2000

A comment piece yesterday, page 23, had Winston Churchill reflecting on his time as a 'profoundly unsuccessful schoolboy at Marlborough'. He went to Harrow.

A classical music review (Philharmonia/Ashkenazy) was printed in error, page 20, August 23. The concert it concerned was given in April.

→ 26 August 2000

A Health article, G2, page 10, August 23, said swimming helped reduce 'high blood pressure and hypertension'. They mean the same thing.

In a piece about a Northern Ireland jail (August 24, early editions, page 2) the ninth word in this sentence should have been not: 'The prison authorities are adamant that they will introduce the policies that resulted in the Maze being run by inmates.'

→ 29 August 2000

A piece on the new musical director of Glyndebourne opera, Vladimir Jurowski, seemed to say his Welsh National Opera production of Hansel and Gretel was staged in Edinburgh (page 8, August 26), whereas it was put on in Covent Garden and Cardiff. The piece also looked ahead to a revival of 'Sir Peter Paul's famous 1985 production' of Albert Herring. That is, Sir Peter Hall.

→ 11 September 2000

The survey referred to in a report, Doctors' warning on head lice chemicals, page 10, September 5, found that 30 percent of respondents thought that regularly using insecticides would ensure children did not catch head lice. It did not find that 30 percent were actually using them in this misguided way.

→ 13 September 2000

In our profile of David James, page 15, September 9, we quoted him saying about the diving support vessel British Argyll: 'That ship was the last built at Smith's yard on Teesside. Any tear-jerking stories you ever hear about the poor workers of Sunderland do not take account of the dreadful manner in which that ship was built.' Sunderland, in fact, had nothing to do with it. Sunderland is not on Teesside but on Wearside. Mr James did not make the mistake. We did. Apologies

→ 14 September 2000

The play at the Almeida in London is Conversations After a Burial, as our review, page 18, yesterday, indicated, and not Conversations After a Funeral as a caption to the accompanying picture said (even though it may amount to the same thing).

We misidentified the two players in our photograph from the Fulham–Burnley match at Craven Cottage, page 31, yesterday. They were not Andy Melville and Ian Cox (as originally captioned by the agency supplying the picture). They were Barry Hayles and Mitchell Thomas. Apologies all round.

→ 15 September 2000

In a column, page 5, G2, yesterday, we appeared to be confusing the Internationale and the Red Flag, quoting from the latter immediately after mentioning the former. We referred to the lyrics by 'James O'Connell'. The lyrics of the Red Flag were written by Jim Connell (1852–1929).

English department, from a column on page 9 (Parents), G2, September 13, ' . . . as if I were any more likely to use this ridiculous fop to world environmental destruction the second time around.' Fop: A man who is excessively concerned with fashion and elegance. (Collins). Sop: a bribe or concession etc, given to placate or mollify (same source).

To give a sop to Cerberus (the three-headed dog at the gates of Hades), 'When persons died the Greeks and Romans used to put a cake in their hands as a sop to Cerberus to allow them to pass without molestation.' (Brewer's Dictionary of Phrase & Fable). See also, the 12th labour of Heracles.

→ **16 September 2000**

Homophone corner, from page 4, G2, September 5, ' . . . his gangly build . . . leant itself to professional basketball . . .'

And, from a letter, page 21, yesterday, 'We . . . drove to the gym [and] worked out on the stationery bike . . .'

→ **18 September 2000**

English department, from a piece about the television programme Big Brother, page 2, G2, September 15, '[She] kept demanding that the evictees ditch the dirt on events in the house.' You can ditch a boyfriend or girlfriend, but you dish the dirt ('spread malicious gossip' Collins).

→ **19 September 2000**

English department, from page 8, Weekend, September 16, where we said, 'The higher you hoist your petard, the more unequivocal its salute . . .', perhaps confusing petard with pennant. The writer is making a distant reference to Shakespeare: Hamlet, III, iv, ' . . .For 'tis sport to have the engineer/ Hoist with his own petard . . .' Brewer's Dictionary of Phrase & Fable defines it thus: 'Beaten with his own weapons, caught in his own trap,' and tells us, 'The petard was a thick iron engine of war, filled with gunpowder, and fastened to gates, barricades, etc, to blow them up. The danger was lest the engineer who fired the petard should be blown up [into the air = hoist, OED] by the explosion.' Petard, probably from the French, peter, break wind.

→ **20 September 2000**

A report about a building complex used for raves on the Baltic coast of Germany (page 8, G2, August 31), carried a headline incorrectly saying that Hitler had had it built as a 'holiday camp for Nazi stormtroopers'. As the text stated, the Nazi regime built it as a holiday place for ordinary workers.

→ 22 September 2000

Spanish department, from an article headed Don't give in Gordon, etc, page 22, September 20, where we said, 'So is the answer to sit tight and just say No Passeran to the truckers?' We should have said No Pasaran (roughly, They shall not pass), a phrase from the Spanish civil war, the siege of Madrid.

→ 28 September 2000

Our conversion of hectares into acres (The messiah of Troina, page 2, G2, yesterday) was wildly out. We divided when we should have multiplied. One hectare is equivalent to 2.471 acres. Therefore, 700 hectares is 1,729.7 acres (not 280) and 1,500 hectares is 3,706.5 acres (not 600).

→ 29 September 2000

Doctors stored the sperm of the profile subject, page 4, G2, September 27, because they feared his condition might leave him infertile, rather than impotent. Impotent: unable to have sexual intercourse; infertile: incapable of producing offspring (Collins).

Danish department, from Pass Notes on Denmark, page 3, G2, yesterday, where we said we had 'a whole smørrebrød of alternative dodgy cultural references'. Dodgy indeed. Smørrebrød is the Danish for sandwich. We probably meant smörgåsbord, which is not Danish, but Swedish for sandwich-table or buffet.

→ 03 September 2000

In recommending Laurence Olivier's Henry V, among the week's best films on television, page 53, the Guide, September 30, we drew particular attention to his 'St Swithin's Day' speech before the battle of Agincourt. We called it 'a heroic rabble-rouser'. It was, of course, St Crispin's Day. This is how the speech, from Act IV, scene iii, concludes: And gentlemen in England, now a-bed /Shall think themselves accurs'd they were not here,/And hold their manhoods cheap whiles any speak/That fought with us upon Saint Crispin's day.

The hurricane warning, page 15 yesterday, covered the Yucatan peninsula, not peninsular (a word very rarely needed but often used).

→ 05 October 2000

In a report headed Mafiaville cheers its anti-mob hero, page 18, October 3, we mistakenly suggested that the Mafia bosses Luciano Liggio and Lucky Luciano were the same person. Luciano Liggio was a Sicilian criminal who became the Mafia chieftain of Corleone. Salvatore Lucania (Lucky Luciano) was boss of the New York family which bore his name. Luciano Liggio, as we said, murdered Placido Rizzotto, the subject of a new anti-Mafia film. The error was in the editing.

→ 07 October 2000

In our lead feature in G2 yesterday about cannabis, we asked people whether they smoked it and quoted the former leader of the SNP, Alex Salmond as saying: 'If you say "yes" people claim you're encouraging and supporting it and if you say "no" it looks like you're a prick.' Mr Salmond has asked us to make it clear that what he actually said was 'prig', not 'prick'.

→ 09 October 2000

Homophone corner, from our obituary of Wojciech Has, page 24, October 5, in which we said a character from one of his films, 'wakes up from sexual ecstasy surrounded by bones and sculls'.

→ 10 October 2000

Margaret Rutherford was not an 'unforgettable Lady Bracknell' (The Guide, page 19, October 7) in Anthony Asquith's film of The Importance of Being Earnest (1952). That was Edith Evans. Margaret Rutherford was unforgettable as Miss Prism.

→ 11 October 2000

The Glasgow thoroughfare referred to in a leader, page 21, yesterday, is Sauchiehall, not Sauciehall.

→ 13 October 2000

In a column, page 5, Weekend, October 7, we spoke of a possible triumph 'for the breast transplant industry'. That would be breast implant.

Homophone corner, from a column on page 20, October 10, in which the writer compared the experience of making love with 'being wrapped lightly across the knuckles with a damp envelope . . .'

→ 14 October 2000

We have been trying to eradicate 'bored of', often mistakenly used instead of bored with or bored by, but it cropped up again in a heading on page 15, G2, October 11. Our style guide has proscribed it.

→ 24 October 2000

The bird captioned 'Nightingale: invisible', page 7, G2, yesterday, is visibly a skylark, as the caption supplied to us clearly said.

In our report about Sir Eduardo Paolozzi, page 6, yesterday, we intended to refer to him as a senior academician (a senior member of the Royal Academy of Arts), rather than as a senior academic.

→ 26 October 2000

In our obituary of Eduard Goldstücker, page 24, yesterday, we said, 'He passionately opposed the distortion of truth and the fortification of history.' Falsification, that should have been. Our mistake.

→ 03 November 2000

Not a homophone, from page 31, November 1, Market forces, 'In Glaxo's case it was further problems with its controversial treatment for irritable bowl syndrome . . .'

→ 04 November 2000

The chimpanzees on the front of Science, November 2, were orang-utans.

→ 06 November 2000

Our reference to the national 'herd' of sheep, a leader, page 23, November 2, should have been to the national flock.

→ 13 November 2000

In our account of Lou Kenton's experiences in the Spanish civil war, page 2, G2, November 10, there was a sentence starting, 'When Khruschev's tanks rolled into Prague . . .' They were Brezhnev's tanks.

→ 17 November 2000

The review of Coronation Street, page 22, G2, November 14 (Tuesday's paper) was, in fact, not a review of Monday's episode but a (p)review of Wednesday's episode. A confusion of review tapes. Apologies.

→ 21 November 2000

In a report headed Stranger than fiction, pages 2 and 3, G2, November 16, about Florida and its way with elections, we said that Carol Roberts, a member of the Palm Beach electoral board, was forced to step down after being charged with ballot-tampering. In fact, she defended herself against the charges and was vindicated. The attempt to unseat her was therefore unsuccessful. In the same piece we said "a man in south-central Florida was charged with shooting his dog because he suspected it of being gay". The reporter who covered the case says the dog, a neutered Yorkshire terrier-poodle cross, was not shot but struck on the head with a plastic piece of a vacuum cleaner, because the owner believed he was attempting an unnatural act with a Jack Russell terrier. The blow fractured the dog's skull and a local veterinary surgeon put the dog down. The dog's owner was sentenced to six months in prison, a term now nearing its end. Finally, Ocala is in north-central Florida, rather than south-central [Thanks to Rick Cundiff of the Ocala Star-Banner].

→ 25 November 2000

A native of Bermuda or a thing associated with Bermuda may be called Bermudian but not Bermudan (Court battle over key Pollock painting, page 5, November 24).

→ **27 November 2000**

In our report, Reckless bush clearance may cost Australia the earth, page 21, November 24, we referred to a couple who acquired 790 hectares of land and said this was equivalent to 320 acres. We should have said they had acquired 320 hectares which was equivalent to 790 acres.

→ **28 November 2000**

In an article on the paperbacks page of the Saturday Review, page 11, November 25, we twice mentioned the new book by Terry Jones and on both occasions got it wrong. We called it The Knight and His Lady, and The Squire and His Lady. It is, in fact, called The Lady and the Squire. The page heading notwithstanding, it is a hardback.

→ **29 November 2000**

The graphic accompanying our report about the misspelling of a tattoo on David Beckham's arm, giving his wife Victoria's name in Hindi, page 1, yesterday, itself had a mistake in it. In transcribing the erroneous tattoo we inserted an extra character, thereby simply adding to the confusion. The fact remains, that the tattoo on Beckham's arm is wrong (but not as wrong as our version).

→ **30 November 2000**

In our obituary of Conrad Voss Bark, whom we described as a journalist and fly-fishing enthusiast, page 24, yesterday, we said his pastimes included typing files. He much preferred tying flies, of course. The obituarist is exonerated.

→ **1 December 2000**

Homophone corner, from Policy and politics, page 10, yesterday, 'Hague . . . appears to be unphased by it all.'

→ **8 December 2000**

In an article, page 22, December 7, we suggested that Summerhouse in England by Van Morrison could be adopted as the new anthem. There is no such track by Van Morrison but there is a Summertime in England.

→ 12 December 2000

From page 3, Media, yesterday: ' . . . even after a fine tooth-comb examination [they] were exonerated'. That would be fine-tooth comb. Collins Millennium: go over with a fine-tooth(ed) comb, to examine very thoroughly.

The lower-case christmas in our note about the Top 10 cookbooks, page 11, Saturday Review, December 9, was just a slip. Christmas still has an initial capital, even in the Guardian.

→ 13 December 2000

Homophone corner, from New Media Diary, page 43, Media, December 11: 'The crowd waited with baited breath . . .'

→ 15 December 2000

A (very) belated correction to a statement in an article And now for the forecast, pages 6 and 7, G2, November 6, in which we said it was the astronomer royal, Sir Harold Spencer Jones, who dismissed the idea of space flight as 'bunk'. It was Sir Richard van der Riet Woolley who, as astronomer royal, made that statement, although he said 'bilge' not 'bunk'.

In a column, page 7, Society, December 13, we said: 'In the words of Lord Rothschild, boss of the former think tank, their role is to produce the grit which creates the oyster.' More valuably, the grit creates the pearl (in some oysters).

→ 20 December 2000

A misprint of 'public' in the Saturday Review, page 2, December 16, resulted in Neville Cardus being quoted as writing on Shaw: 'We had been repressed so long in our pubic discussions . . . an hour of it and not a fumble.'

→ 4 January 2001

The recipes for a long, lazy lunch to revive the spirits after the holiday festivities, pages 32 and 33, Weekend, December 30, were all for 20 people rather than the six we said they served. Apologies to readers who already have an excess of lamb korma on their hands.

→ 10 January 2001

The Colombian officer overseeing the police operation described on pages 8 and 9, G2, January 8, was Colonel Bonilla, rather than Colonial Bonilla.

→ 18 January 2001

In a report headed Anger at plan to dump bags of depleted uranium, page 7, yesterday, we said that BNFL was to dump 30,000 bags of nuclear waste containing depleted uranium, at a site three miles from Preston, 'in the river Ribble'. Less alarmingly, and more accurately, it should have said, beside or near the river Ribble.

→ 20 January 2001

The details of Derek Malcolm's new book, page 5, G2, January 18, were correct except for the title, publisher and price. The book is A Century of Films: Derek Malcolm's Personal Best (not Derek Malcolm's Personal Best: A Century of Films). The publisher's name is IB Tauris (not ID Tauris), but more specifically the imprint is Tauris Parke Paperbacks. The price is £9.99 not £9.95.

→ 22 January 2001

Homophone corner, from page 15, Friday Review, January 19, where we spoke of a 'totalitarian society based on fundamentalist religious principals'. This overworked homophone is mentioned again as a matter of principle.

→ 23 January 2001

A descendant of the marine archaeologist Franck Goddio could not have taken part in the Battle of the Nile in 1798, Today's TV, G2, page 24, January 22, although one of his ancestors could have been there.

→ 24 January 2001

All three photographs, of works by Caravaggio and Carracci, accompanying an article about The Genius of Rome 1592–1623 exhibition at the Royal Academy, G2, page 12, yesterday, were accidentally reversed.

→ 30 January 2001

In a report headed £4.5bn on offer to revive rail service, page 13, January 25, we said, 'Tourists pouring off the Channel ferries or approaching London on Eurostar from Paris or Brussels have expressed their shock at seeing such a rundown station [Clapham Junction] at the southern gateway to the capital'. None of these services goes to or through Clapham Junction.

Homophone corner, from an article headed Farewell, focus groupie, page 22, Comment, January 27: 'The people cleaning out Peter Mandelson's offices at Labour party headquarters had a bit of a shock when they unlocked the stationary cupboard.'

→ 1 February 2001

In a radio review, page 20, G2, January 29, we said, confusingly: 'A widower told of the treatment her husband had received . . .'
f2 February 2001

Homophone corner, from page 7, Small business solutions, with yesterday's Guardian: 'We new nothing about Wap, they new nothing about Wap . . .'

→ 6 February 2001

In a review of a book about Palestine under the British mandate, Books, page 8, Saturday Review, February 3, we made CP Snow the editor of the Manchester Guardian, allowing him, embarrassingly, to usurp the position of the Guardian's most famous editor, CP Scott. The writer of the review was, as we said, Colin Shindler, the author of Israel, Likud and the Zionist Dream, not to be confused with Colin Shindler, the author of Manchester United Ruined My Life, who also writes for the Guardian. The Guardian itself must take all the responsibility for allowing this particular mistake to reach the printed page.

→ 7 February 2001

'Mary Shelley's Dracula', mentioned in a column, page 5, G2, yesterday, is, of course, Bram Stoker's. Mary Shelley wrote Frankenstein.

From a report, page 24, Finance, February 3: 'He trained as a dentist for two years but gave up to join Littlewoods as a stock controller in charge of ankle stocks.'

→ 8 February 2001

The song by Gabriel Fauré, Au cimetière, composed and published in 1888, became Au cinematière in our radio listings, page 73, the Guide, February 3 (Radio 3, Monday 1pm).

→ 13 February 2001

In our piece about the exhibition of Italian paintings of the 18th century, Settecento: Tiepolo's Century, at Lille, page 11, G2, yesterday, we mentioned Guardi's 'Emmaus's Supper' and went on to speak of the painting as though Emmaus were the name of a man rather than a village 'outside Jerusalem' (Luke, ch 24, verses 13–35). Paintings of the subject are usually called The Supper at Emmaus. The famous Venetian church Santa Maria della Salute is usually referred to by that name in French as it is, also, in English.

The moray patterns, referred to in a caption on page 47, Weekend, February 10, are moiré patterns.

→ 14 February 2001

In our account of the Game Spirit Chase at Newbury, page 10, Sport, February 12, all references to Foundry Lane should have been made instead to Function Dream.

→ 15 February 2001

In a panel headed Great railway feats, page 3, February 10, Kapiri Mposhi in Zambia was spelt wrongly and we were woefully out on its distance from Dar es Salaam in Tanzania. The Tazara rail line between the two places is 1,139 miles long and not 2,900 miles as stated.

→ 17 February 2001

Small point from an article about race and The Archers, page 6, G2, yesterday, xenophobia is spelt with an x not a z.

→ 20 February 2001

The scientist referred to near the end of our profile of EO Wilson, pages 6 and 7, Review, February 17, is Sarah Hrdy (not Hardy), the author of The Woman That Never Evolved and Mother Nature.

→ 21 February 2001

The article headed Wanna be a pop star? Education, pages 10 and 11, yesterday, does make sense but only if the columns are read in the following order: 1,4,2,3,5,6,7. Apologies.

→ 22 February 2001

In an article on page 2 of the Science section, February 15, we said: 'Out of more than 4,000 types of amphibians we have reproductive information on a handful of species. The variation is enormous: blind snakes .. . sea snakes . . . crocodiles . . .' None of these is an amphibian. They are all reptiles. London Zoo says so.

→ 23 February 2001

Cardinal Cormac Murphy-O'Connor's new biretta became a beretta in a caption to a photograph of the papal kiss, page 14, yesterday. Collins dictionary allows berretta with a double r as an alternative (the Italian spelling). The Spanish spelling is birreta, one t. Beretta in the spelling we used in the caption is the name of an Italian gun manufacturer.

→ 1 March 2001

In a report headed Drink and assault sealed fate of hangman's butcher, page 11, February 24, we said Albert Pierrepoint was the last executioner in Britain. He was not. Pierrepoint's period in office ended in 1956. Harry Allen and Robert Leslie Stewart simultaneously dispatched the last two men hanged in Britain, at Strangeways and Walton, on August 13, 1964.

→ 2 March 2001

In an article about gap years, Education, pages 12 and 13, February 27, we included in a survival guide for students working abroad the advice to 'get vaccinated against illnesses like TB and malaria'. There is no vaccination against malaria.

→ 3 March 2001

In a panel listing events that have been, or could be, postponed because of foot and mouth disease restrictions, we included the following: 'Britain's oldest horse race, the Derby, faces cancellation for only the second time in its 480-year history.' The Derby is not Britain's oldest horse race. Britannica.com, pointing out that the modern age of racing began with the inauguration of the English classic races, lists them in the following order: the St Leger, 1776; the Oaks, 1779; the Derby, 1780; (all of them falling a long way short of 480 years of age).

→ 5 March 2001

In a piece headed The perils of loyalty, page 22 (Comment), March 1, we referred to 'the moral satin of Clinton's career'. That should have read 'the moral stain' etc.

→ 7 March 2001

In a letter in Weekend, page 5, March 3, we had the writer say 'the average glass of milk contains 112,899,408-plus cells'. That should have been pus cells.

→ 14 March 2001

A standfirst to a story about barristers, page 3, March 8, said: 'Lawyers rile at report claiming they break trading rules.' This report clearly riled some lawyers – but our construction should have read, 'Lawyers rail at report'.

→ 20 March 2001

A headline on the lead story in the Saturday Review, March 17, was stretching a point when it said that the artist Stanley Spencer visited China 'just before the Cultural Revolution'. Spencer visited China, as the piece said, in 1954. He died in 1959, still well before the beginning of the Cultural Revolution in 1966.

→ 23 March 2001

The world's first McDonald's hotel is not at Rümland in Switzerland (page 14, March 16), or Ramlüng (pages 6, G2, March 19) but Rümlang.

→ 24 March 2001

The reader who promised a deferential touch of her fetlock, Letters, page 21, yesterday, would probably be touching, or tugging, her forelock.

→ 2 April 2001

In a report about the 'euthanasia drug', pentobarbitone sodium, page 4, March 30, we made several references to 100 millimetre bottles. We meant to refer to millilitres.

The words that Bessie Smith sang (page 16, G2, March 28) were 'Give me [or Gimme] a pigfoot and a bottle of beer . . .' not the terser 'Gimme a pigfoot and a beer . . .'

→ 5 April 2001

In an article headed Our survey said . . ., pages 8 and 9, G2, April 2, we suggested that the lighthouse at 'Athens harbour' was one of the wonders of the world. It was not, but the lighthouse at Alexandria was. Here is the list: The great pyramid of Giza, the hanging gardens of Babylon, the statue of Zeus at Olympia, the temple of Artemis at Ephesus, the mausoleum at Halicarnassus, the Colossus of Rhodes, and the lighthouse of Alexandria.

→ 6 April 2001

The husband of the Countess of Wessex, page 1, yesterday, is not the Count of Wessex. He is the Earl of Wessex.

→ 10 April 2001

In an obituary of John Ardoin, the music critic, page 20, yesterday, we said the most important of his four books on Maria Callas, The Callas Legacy, 'analysed all her recordings in scrumptious detail'. We meant to say 'scrupulous detail'.

→ 19 April 2001

The dolphins did not talk (Net deaths put species at risk, page 11, April 14) in spite of the impression given by our caption, which said that bottlenose dolphins were 'in urgent need of conversation measures'. It is conservation that is needed, particularly in the Moray Firth, which we incorrectly called the Murray Firth.

Geography department (1): In Weatherwatch, page 16, April 17, Ahmadabad was placed in northeast India. It is a city in Gujarat, which is in west-central India.

Geography department (2): Cape Verde Islands (Paint it black, G2, page 14, April 16) lie 200 miles west of Senegal, in the Atlantic. We said they were 200 miles to the east, which would place them inland, on the border between Mali and Mauritania.

Geography department (3): If Childe Harold had travelled downstream on the Rhine from Königswinter (He wrote the poem, you see the sights, Travel, page 2, April 14) he would have ended up in Rotterdam instead of Koblenz. He would also have noticed that the lake in Hamburg is called Alster and not Alstadt, that Drachenfels has just one l, that Siebengebirge (the seven hills) are not Sibengerberge, and that Hatto was archbishop of Mainz, not Meinz.

→ 20 April 2001

Star of the definitive 1952 western, High Noon, was Gary Cooper, not Cary Grant (Godfather bows out of Lloyds after 49 years, page 24, April 19).

→ 21 April 2001

In the obituary of David Lloyd Owen, page 18, April 16, we said that in later life he was chairman of the Wildflowers Association of Great Britain. This should have read 'wildfowlers'.

→ 26 April 2001

Homophone corner: an unfamiliar sound on the District and Circle lines (Human traffic, G2, page 4, April 23) as someone 'pulled the passenger emergency chord'.

→ 30 April 2001

In our G2 cover story, All the president's businessmen, April 27, Johns Hopkins University in Baltimore, one of the more famous universities of the US, once again became John Hopkins.

A brief item about a replica in Florida of Michelangelo's David having to wear a loincloth after complaints by people living nearby carried the headline 'David doffs a loin cloth' in early editions, April 26. It became, more correctly, 'David dons a loin cloth' for later editions.

→ 1 May 2001

More than a few readers noticed that the shipwrecked people on The Raft of the Medusa, the painting by Gericault, page 9, Saturday Review, April 28, were sailing in the wrong direction. The picture, the original of which is in the Louvre, was accidentally reversed.

→ 4 May 2001

Peter Sansom, one of the judges of the Online text poetry competition, pages 10 and 11, Online, yesterday, referred to the haiku as Chinese rather than Japanese, an aberration for which he apologises.

→ 12 May 2001

In our Face to faith column, page 22, April 28, we said: 'At the end of his life, Saint Thomas Aquinas . . . came to see that faced with God, his Summa Theologica – and all his writings – were not straw.' On the contrary, he came to see that they were straw.

→ 14 May 2001

A feature marking the feast day of St Apollonius and warning against possible confusion with other saints similarly named, page 18, G2, April 18, was illustrated with a detail of mosaic showing St Aphthonios, who had nothing to do with the story at all.

→ 15 May 2001

In our obituary of RK Narayan, page 22, yesterday, we said that Graham Greene 'energetically sang his prodigee's praises', thus spelling wrongly a word that would, in any case, have been inappropriate. A prodigy is a person, especially a child, of marvellous talents. Whereas a protégé, the sense intended here, is a person protected and aided by the patronage of another (definitions from Collins).

Pharaoh, a word commonly misspelt – as pharoah – appeared wrongly again in a heading and caption on page 7, yesterday (a report headed Pyramids seen as stairways to heaven). It was correct in the report itself. A reader suggests 'arse over head' as a useful mnemonic.

→ 16 May 2001

Recurring homophone, from page 3, May 14: 'The minority channel [Channel 4] lauded it over the BBC and ITV ….'

→ 23 May 2001

An After hours item on the benefits of tango dancing (Page 16, Office Hours, May 21) said: 'Once you are proficient, wardrobe is of tantamount importance.' That would be paramount.

Our obituary on page 24 yesterday of Sam Sherry, acrobatic dancer, clog dancer and singer, said: 'His slight fame always belied the energy and excitement of his dancing.' The intention was, frame.

→ 29 May 2001

Notwithstanding the militarised state of the Holy Land at present, a reader rightly challenged our reference – Taking the tablets, Page 12, Society, May 23 – to the 'Ten Commandants'.

→ 30 May 2001

A reference to intercontinental Eurostar trains, French set record … page 9, May 28, should have said 'international'.

→ 31 May 2001

Our 'At home' roundup, page 3, the Editor, May 26, included a reference to a 'silicon-enhanced model'. On page 6 of the same issue of the Editor, we said the woman in question was 'famous for having more silicon than . . . Silicon Valley'. What she perhaps has is silicone, the compound commonly used for breast implants. Silicon Valley is correct .

→ **7 June 2001**

Homophone corner, from page 7, G2, June 5: 'At Blenheim, he . . . damned a small river to create a lake.'

→ **8 June 2001**

The statue in Winchester referred to in an election sketch on our front page yesterday represents Alfred the Great, not William the Conqueror.

→ **9 June 2001**

In the Society section cover story, Talking rubbish, June 6, we referred to Dudley council having an excellent 'best value' report for its refuse collection service. In fact it was Oldham council that had the good service. The council official Mike Kelly mentioned in the report works for Oldham, not Dudley, and all the details of the contract referred to Oldham and not Dudley.

→ **12 June 2001**

A column headed We all love Labour – aren't we nice?, page 27, June 9, referred to Tony Blair's 'defiant way of . . . sending his children to fee-paying schools'. Just to be clear about it, the Oratory is not a fee-paying school.

→ **13 June 2001**

Shakespeare went awry in a column, page 9, G2, yesterday, in which John Prescott and Ann Widdecombe were seen as 'the Viola and Sebastian of politics – Twelfth Night twins fatefully separated at birth'. In fact they were separated in a shipwreck on the shores of Illyria.

→ **18 June 2001**

The caption to a picture of Anita Roddick, used to illustrate an article headed Ethics woman seeks a makeover, page 28 (Finance), June 8, mistakenly placed her in Guyana, on the north-eastern corner of South America, instead of Ghana in western Africa where the picture was taken.

→ **19 June 2001**

English department (1), from page 5, Media, yesterday, 'those [journalists] who went there [the Westminster lobby] via public school and Oxbridge remain under the delusion that all architecture is gothic, all deserts are served with custard . . .' 'Desserts' that would be.

English department (2), from page 9, G2 (Style), June 15, where we referred to 'the most subtle (and therefore incredibly expensive) leather imaginable'. 'Most supple' that would be.

English department (3), from a report, page 8, yesterday, in which we passed on a warning from the former culture secretary, Chris Smith, that the government should not allow itself to fall 'in hoc' to Rupert Murdoch. The English expression is 'in hock', not to be confused with the Latin ad hoc, which means something completely different.

English department (4), page 20, G2, yesterday, 'their's'.

→ **25 June 2001**

A paragraph at the end of our report, Prodi anxious to allay Irish worries, page 14, June 22, had Herr Schröder addressing the Reichstag. He was talking to the Bundestag which is now housed in the Reichstag.

The unwanted apostrophe, from a heading G2, page 2, June 22: 'There was just one catch: the sex. Lot's of it.'

→ **26 June 2001**

We replaced the picture of the England v Australia game at the Oval for the final edition, page 32, June 22, but the caption remained unchanged giving the impression that we did not know one team from the other. We do.

→ **28 June 2001**

The father of Jelena Dokic, page 33 (Sport), June 27, inadvertently flouted (not flaunted) Wimbledon's no smoking rule by flaunting (not flouting) his pipe.

→ 13 July 2001

In a report headed Library is a closed book for schools, page 5, yesterday, we referred to 'the Roman historian Herodotus'. Herodotus was a Greek historian.

→ 18 July 2001

A brief report headed Dane drifts to Norway, page 13, early editions, yesterday, began: 'A German who put to sea in Denmark ... while drunk awoke to find himself drifting off the coast of Norway.' The heading was changed for later editions.

→ 24 July 2001

The picture captioned Grand Canyon, page 8, Saturday Review, July 21 (the page after the readers' editor's article on mistakes involving pictures), was not the Grand Canyon. It was Monument Valley, NE Arizona/SE Utah.

In an article headed Don't worry, mate, it's on expenses, page 10 (Work), G2, July 10, we referred to the 'US-owned Dresdner Kleinwort Wasserstein'. It is, of course, a European bank.

The university in Baltimore is Johns Hopkins, not John Hopkins as it appeared on the Books pages (page 9) of the Saturday Review, July 21: a tedious error.

→ 26 July 2001

Homophone corner from page 30, Sport, yesterday: Sir Alex Ferguson last night unveiled a third ... player to compliment Ruud van Nistelrooy and Juan Veron ...

→ 27 July 2001

In an article about the meeting of George W Bush and the Pope (July 25), we said that Mr Bush presided over 112 executions as governor of Texas. Amnesty points out that the correct figure for executions during his gubernatorial reign is 152.

→ 28 July 2001

Lady Macbeth of Mtsensk, having appeared in the Guardian as Lady Macbeth of Minsk (July 3), became Lady Macbeth of Mtensk (page 14, G2, July 24).

→ 30 July 2001

In a piece about the beer industry in Germany, page 24, Finance, July 25, Humorator became Humerator; Binding became Bundung; and Brau und Brunnen became Brau und Binnen.

It is not Morecombe Bay (a graphic, Health authority waiting lists, page 11, July 26). It is Morecambe Bay. Morecambe and Morecambe Bay are now usually spelt correctly (wrong about 10 times in the past two years, and right about 300).

→ 31 July 2001

A misprint, from page 21, Jobs & Money, July 28: 'Railtrack was able to embark on a viscous circle of underinvestment leading to delays and train collisions . . .'

→ 2 August 2001

In our guide to the Premier league transfers, page 26 (Sport), yesterday, we said Guillaume Norbert of Arsenal had gone to Leyton Orient. He has gone to the French club Lorient.

→ 8 August 2001

It is not correct to describe the Minotaur as 'one of Europa's grandchildren', page 14, G2 (Arts), July 25. The Minotaur was the offspring of Pasiphae, the wife of Europa's son, Minos, and a bull which Minos should have sacrificed to Poseidon. Minos, in any biological sense, had nothing to do with it.

→ 13 August 2001

The headline, One in every nine South Africans murdered, page 9, August 10, was misleading. As the copy made clear, 'one in nine of all deaths [each year] . . . are murder'.

→ 15 August 2001

The Caribbean island of Nelson, Exiled to paradise, Saturday Review, page 3, August 11, was described as 'a square mile in circumference'. The area of the island may be one square mile but its circumference has to be a linear measure.

→ 29 August 2001

In our leader on the funding of science research, Who pays the piper? page 15, August 27, we said that the aorta carries blood to the heart when in fact it carries blood away from the heart.

→ 1 September 2001

Spell check: complimentary newspaper, not complementary (Them and us, G2, page 2, yesterday); fluoride, not flouride (Tooth decay worst among children in the north, page 10, yesterday); women's not womens' (four times in Battle of the Tory wives, G2, page 6, August 30); defuse trouble, not diffuse (Gentle touch to pacify England fans, page 5, August 30); Colosseum or Coliseum but not Colloseum (Romance in ruins, page 17, August 30); Cobholm in Yarmouth, not Cobham (On the road to Yarmouth pier, Saturday Review, page 12, August 25); Gypsy, not gypsy (The Guide, Clubs, page 28, August 25); affected even the humble cyclist, not effected (Country Diary, page 16, August 24).

→ 6 September 2001

Mousse trap, from page 9 (Women), September 3: '. . . the hostess produced a tunafish ring, made in a jelly mould, the top filled with egg mouse . . .'

→ 10 September 2001

The golliwog was banished from Robertson's jam labels, not Robinson's (Golliwog stunt leaves Tory in a jam, page 2, September 6).

→ 20 September 2001

A columnist, wrote as follows on page 6, G2, yesterday: 'In the Times, Michael Gove has devised the word "Guardianistas", for the pantywaists (nervous nellies) who read this paper . . .' The columnist saw in the word the imputation of effeminacy and said, 'Me, I'm a Guardianisto . . .' In fact, there is nothing feminine or effeminate in Spanish -ista endings which indicate neuter nouns as in periodista (Spanish for journalist).

→ 6 October 2001

The map accompanying our report of the Russian airliner disaster, on the front page yesterday, was wrong in a number of important points. It showed Novosibirsk, the capital of Siberia, as a resort on the Black Sea. It showed Israel extending over Jordan, and Jordan in place of Iraq.

An article, Fowl play, on page 7, G2, yesterday, about pheasants was illustrated by a man banging away on a grouse moor.

→ 8 October 2001

In relating a week in the life of the poet Sean O'Brien, page 19, G2, October 5, we (rather than he) managed to make North Shields one word, and Wallsend two.

→ 10 October 2001

The boy reciting the Koran, in a dispatch from Afghanistan, page 4, yesterday, had his eyes painted not with 'black coal' but with kohl. 'Kohl: a cosmetic powder used, originally esp. in Muslim and Asian countries, to darken the area around the eyes.' (Collins Millennium edition).

In an article headed They came in search of paradise, page 14, G2, October 8, we said that the film star Robert Donat was a Hungarian. He was born in Withington, Manchester, in 1905. His father was Polish.

Homophone corner, from a television review, page 22, G2, October 8: ' . . . money can quite obviously buy you anything you like [including] diamonds in the souls of your hiking boots . . .'

→ 17 October 2001

In a brief item headed The force is made a religion, page 14, October 11, we said that 'Jedi' had been coded to appear in the next census because so many people gave it as their religion in the recent census. The Office for National Statistics says that is not the case. It points out that questions for the census are set by parliament and it says that it is beyond the bounds of likelihood that 'Jedi Knight' will be included in any future census. Any Jedi Knights will be listed as 'other'.

→ **20 October 2001**

In a report on page 6 (Israel tells Arafat to hand over minister's assassins), October 18, we identified Yossi Sarid as the leader of 'the rightwing Meretz party'. On page 7 (Far right leader who fell victim to his own ideas), the same day, we said Yossi Sarid was leader of 'the leftwing Meretz party'. The latter is correct .

→ **22 October 2001**

In a caption to a picture accompanying a report of the appointment of a new artistic director for the Bayreuth Festival we said he might raise a few eyebrows 'as well as arias'. There are no arias in Wagner's Ring.

→ **25 October 2001**

In our edited version of Mr Blair's speech on the IRA's act of decommissioning, page 5, yesterday, we had him say: 'All parliamentary organisations should follow suit.' It was paramilitary organisations he was advising to take that course rather than parliamentary ones.

In a report headed A far pavilion where the Taliban lose at cricket, page 10, October 16, we mistakenly said that Afghanistan had become in June an associate member of the International Cricket Council (ICC). In fact, it only became an affiliate member.

→ **29 October 2001**

In a continuation of Online's lead feature, page 3, October 25, we said: 'Chelsea is toying with the idea of offering whole games live several hours after the final whistle.'

→ **31 October 2001**

In an agency report, £25m plot to 'blackmail' Barclays, early editions page 2, later editions page 10, yesterday, we said: 'He was head of the inscription team . . . responsible for devising code patterns for bank cards.' That would be encryption.

→ 5 November 2001

There are even earlier precedents than Captain Marryat (1836) for the nurse who excused her illegitimate child by saying, 'If you please, ma'am, it was a very little one' (Corrections, November 1). In an Oxford jestbook of 1638, Gratiae Ludentes, a man defends a woman's reputation by saying, 'Indeed, she had a child, but it was a very little one.' This and a prototype from 13th century Syria are cited in John Wardroper's Jest Upon Jest, A Selection from the Jestbooks and Collections of Merry Tales published from the Reign of Richard III to George III (Routledge & Kegan Paul, 1970).

→ 15 November 2001

The cat identified as an Abyssinian, page 47, Weekend, was, in fact, a chocolate tabby-point Siamese. Siamese have blue eyes, Abyssinians do not.

In a letter to the editor, page 23, yesterday, we allowed the writer to say that the English class system had become a social stratification based on 'class by annunciation'. Enunciation, the writer meant to say.

→ 16 November 2001

In an article headed Bushmen aim for cactus rich pickings, page 21, November 10, we said that the Komani people of the Kalahari in southern Africa had 'for thousands of years eaten slices of a six-foot cactus [Hoodia] to stave off hunger on hunting trips'. Hoodia is not a member of the cactus family. It is a member of the Asclepiad family which is a diverse group of succulent and nonsucculent plants found all round the world. The cactus is native to the Americas. See www.cactus-mall.com for a link to the International Asclepiad Society and further information.

→ 24 November 2001

The writer of a column about mispelling, including his own inability to spell, page 5, G2, yesterday, sympathised with Dan Quayle's 'infamous' gaffe in adding an e to tomato. He did not. He added an e to potato (potatoe).

[Misspelling is misspelt in this correction, as a reader quickly pointed out.]

→ 26 November 2001

In a review of a Pulp concert, page 16, November 20, we referred to the 'moribund dry wit' of Jarvis Cocker. We meant to say mordant. (Moribund: near death, without force or vitality mordant: sarcastic, caustic, pungent – Collins dictionary).

→ 6 December 2001

The naming convention for these islands raised itself again yesterday in our leader, A punt on the euro, page 19, when the term 'mainland' was used, twice, to distinguish Great Britain from Northern Ireland. It may be true that the name can be used for the greater part of a single political entity but the long history of disagreement and war surrounding the relationship between the two largest islands in the group clearly renders the concept impolitic. Just over a year ago we said in this column, 'We think "mainland" is insupportable'.

The skink is not a rodent, it is a reptile (One family and other animals, page 1, early editions, December 4).

→ 11 December 2001

The former director of the National Theatre is Richard Eyre, not Eyres (Northern light heads south, page 11, December 7). In the same piece we mentioned a JB Priestley play, Johnson over Johnson. The correct title is Johnson over Jordan.

→ 24 December 2001

We were wrong to say in our interview, page 13, G2, December 17: 'Loretta Swit has pretty good lips, too. So much so that during the 11 years she played Major Margaret Houlihan in the US sitcom M*A*S*H they gave the character her nickname.' In fact, the character of Major Houlihan had the nickname Hot Lips before Loretta Swit played it. The TV series of M*A*S*H was filmed between 1972–1983, but in the film version, made in 1970, the character of Major Houlihan is played not by Ms Swit but by Sally Kellerman, and the nickname is acquired during the film (her lover Major Burns addresses her thus, unaware that their passionate endearments are being broadcast over the camp's PA system).

→ 3 January 2002

Typographical errors subverted two points made by Martin Rees in 'A brief history of the future', page 1, Saturday Review, December 29. 'We now suspect that atoms live for "only" 1,036 years,' the Astronomer Royal wrote. That was meant to be 10 to the power of 36 (1036). Illustrating another point, he cited the proposition that an infinite series can have a finite sum. But instead of the baffling $1 + H + G \ldots = 2$ the example should have been given as $1 + 1/2 + 1/4 \ldots = 2$.

→ 7 January 2002

The Diary, page 14, January 1, referred to Golden Jubilee street parties held the 'length and breath of the land'. Inventive, but for the orthodox, it's breadth.

→ 11 January 2002

Hatchepsut (Hatshepsut), the pharaoh referred to on page 9 (Parents), G2, January 9, was a queen, not a king.

Contrary to what we said in a column headed Return of the living dead, page 19, yesterday, HMS Hampshire did not sink after hitting a land mine. They are rarely found at sea.

In yesterday's issue of The Wrap, one of our free email services, we referred to mines on the India-Pakistan border being buried 'as deep as three miles underground'. Page 1 of the paper and Guardian Unlimited expressed it more accurately, as 'minefields up to three miles deep' – that is wide or across.

→ 12 January 2002

In our television review, page 18, G2, yesterday, we suggested that Cecil Parkinson was portrayed as a slug by Spitting Image. In fact, that was Kenneth Baker.

A possibly embarrassing mistake slipped into our column, A life inside, page 7, G2, January 10. The passage, 'Del who slimes and grasps my hand firmly,' should have read, 'Del, who smiles etc.'

→ 15 January 2002

A picture, page 13, the Editor, January 12, showed Jutta Kleinschmidt driving through the Mauritanian desert not 'the Mauritian desert'.

Mauritania is in northern Africa. Mauritius is in the Indian Ocean.

The university in Baltimore is Johns Hopkins, not John Hopkins. It appeared wrongly in a leader, page 17, January 12. It is a persistent error.

→ 16 January 2002

The abrasion sustained by President Bush in his pretzel-induced fall, page 1 yesterday, was near his left eye as the picture clearly showed, and not as the text contrarily suggested, under his right eye.

The former heroine addict, page 4, Office Hours, January 14, was a former heroin addict.

→ 18 January 2002

It was wrong to refer to The Beautiful Game (page 5, January 16) as the West End's 'first casualty of September 11'. It closed on September 1.

Bedbound, the play reviewed on page 16, January 16, is not at the National Theatre as we incorrectly stated. It is at the Royal Court Upstairs. The box office number was correct.

→ 21 January 2002

An article headed Marie Skinner had a farm, page 8, Women, January 17, produced a crop of errors. It referred to bone drafts and skin drafts, instead of grafts, it had escaliered trees instead of espaliered, someone was bailing rather than baling, hay it spoke of tennant farmers not tenant. . . .

→ 22 January 2002

Our efforts to spell Lady Macbeth of Mtsensk correctly continue. She appeared to come from 'Mtsenk' on page 12, Saturday Review, January 19.

Readers will have noticed that the leech shown with a posterior sucker at each of its ends in the Guardian house advertisement running recently (see page 20, January 21), has after numerous complaints been, so to speak, rectified. It appeared yesterday with a posterior sucker at one end and an anterior sucker at the other. The advertisement was for the Guardian's website guardian.co.uk

→ 25 January 2002

In our piece about 'fossil meteorites', page 10 (Science), Online, yesterday, we said: 'One meteorite reputably sits directly on top of a trilobite fossil . . .' We meant to say 'reputedly sits' etc.

→ 26 January 2002

In a conflict over the health service, the Tories accused Labour of 'shroud waving', not 'shroud-weaving' (a column, page 21, yesterday).

→ 29 January 2002

Not a correction, but a note to a letter, page 17, yesterday, enlisting EE Cummings (or ee cummings) in the argument about capitalisation. From the New York Times Manual of Style and Usage (Allan M Siegal and William G Connolly): 'Cummings, EE (not ee cummings). Except in his poetry, he used conventional capitalisation.'

We persistently misuse the word fulsome. In a leader, Blair steps up for the public services, page 21, January 26, we said, 'Yesterday was certainly not the first time that Tony Blair has nailed his political colours to the mast on public services. But the speech . . . delivered in Newcastle was the first time . . . that he has done it so extensively, so prominently and so fulsomely.' We meant something like 'wholeheartedly', or 'thoroughly', but that is not what fulsome/ly means. As the Guardian style guide says, it means 'cloying, excessive, disgusting by excess'.

→ 1 February 2002

In our report about the ICA, page 2, January 30, we referred to the famous knitter in A Tale of Two Cities as Madame Lafarge. She was Madame Defarge.

→ 4 February 2002

Homophone corner, from a report from Afghanistan, page 14, January 24: At Ismail Khan's headquarters, men in uniform apply a fresh coat of green paint to the ceremonial canon at the gates.

→ 8 February 2002

In our report about the sale of paintings donated to the Saint Francis of

Assisi Foundation, page 11, February 5, we wrongly referred to the Franciscan friars as monks and in the heading too – Monks raise £11m from painting sale.

→ 9 February 2002

The surgical removal of the clitoris is a clitoridectomy, not a clitorectomy (page 4, G2, yesterday).

→ 11 February 2002

In our page about pilgrimages, Resources, Key stage 2, for pupils from 7 to 11 (page 60, Education, February 5), we referred to Lourdes as a place of 'medieval pilgrimage'. Pilgrimages to Lourdes date only from the 19th century. Saint Bernadette, Bernadette Soubirous, was born there on January 7, 1844, and saw the first apparition of the Virgin Mary in 1858.

→ 12 February 2002

In our piece about William Beckford, page 5, Saturday Review, February 9, we said, 'He never went to Rome. . . .' In fact, Beckford spent many months in Rome. What the writer had said was, 'he never went over to Rome' – that is, he never converted to Catholicism.

→ 19 February 2002

A column on Page 5, Jobs and Monday, February 16 – How shabby are you, Halifax? – referred to fears that major building societies are cocking 'a snoop' at the ombudsman. The gesture of contempt (thumb to nose, and fingers spread out) is known as cocking a snook.

→ 20 February 2002

A letter, page 23, February 16, argued that the time had come to bury the transport ministry. 'A Ministry of Logistics could replace the passive transport,' the writer suggested, 'and a small statute be erected to Jo Moore at some minor but iconic railway centre . . . to mark her contribution.' A statue was probably intended.

→ 22 February 2002

Our correction, page 19, February 19, referring to fears that 'building societies' were cocking a snoop/snook at the financial ombudsman seemed to suggest that the Halifax was a building society. It is not. It is a bank.

→ 26 February 2002

It was not Queen Victoria, who said 'My Lord, I had forgot the fart,' as we seemed to imply, Weekend, page 24, February 23. It was Queen Elizabeth I to Edward de Vere, Earl of Oxford (1550–1604) on his return to court after seven years of self-imposed exile after breaking wind in the royal presence (John Aubrey, Brief Lives).

→ 27 February 2002

In our look at the Laugharne of Dylan Thomas, page 12, Travel, February 23, we had Molly Garter among the characters of Under Milk Wood. We meant Polly Garter (perhaps we were thinking of Molly Bloom).

→ 1 March 2002

The flatworm is not Pseudocerus bifircus (page 5, G2, February 27). It is Pseudoceros bifurcus.

→ 5 March 2002

In Country Diary, page 16, March 1, we said that the horses used by Northumbria Police were chosen 'for temperament and confirmation'. That should have said 'conformation'.

→ 14 March 2002

Homophone of the month, from Country Diary, page 20, G2, yesterday: 'This was the moon, on the first spring tide, to summon up the Severn Boar, the wave which charges inland. . . .'

→ 16 March 2002

It is Sir John Nott, the former defence secretary, who has just published his memoirs – Here Today, Gone Tomorrow. It is Nott not Knott, as it incorrectly appeared in yesterday's Diary, page 22.

→ **19 March 2002**

In Past notes, page 20, yesterday, we said, 'Sadly, Descartes never had a bus company, thus robbing the world of the slogan: "Putting the Carthusian before the horse."' That should have been 'the Cartesian before the horse'. Carthusian: a member of a monastic order founded by Saint Bruno (Collins). Cartesian: relating to the works of Descartes.

→ **20 March 2002**

In a Country Diary headed Branching out, page 16, G2, March 18, we gave the impression that the blackthorn tree produces damsons. Bitter experience confirms that it produces the sloe.

→ **25 March 2002**

In a piece headed Mothers' pride, page 8 (Women), G2, March 21, we referred to a group of women who met in a village on the 'Oxford/ Hertfordshire borders.' Those counties do not have a common border.

→ **3 April 2002**

A feature on Whitby abbey and its new visitor centre in North Yorkshire referred to Atlantic gales battering the site, page 10, G2, April 1. Whatever the paths of the wind, Whitby is on the North sea coast.

→ **16 April 2002**

In a report, ITV looks to £3m crime 'banker', page 9, yesterday, we referred to the judge, John Dredd. The BBC series to which we meant to refer was Judge John Deed. Judge Dredd is a character in the sci-fi comic 2000AD.

→ 17 April 2002

In Rhubarb, rhubarb, the column of arts quotes, page 13, G2, yesterday, we misattributed remarks made by Vittorio Sgarbi, the Italian cultural under-secretary and art historian, to Nanni Moretti, the film director. It was Mr Sgarbi who said, 'I don't think cinema and theatre are essential to humanity. . . .'

The Miles Davis album referred to in Pills and thrills (Friday Review, page 2, April 12) is Sketches of Spain, not Sketches of Pain.

→ 22 April 2002

In a report headed Cows forced to fly after hoofing it to island, page 10, April 19, we said 'The Charolais, a breed [of cattle] that dates back to jurassic times . . . ' That would suggest that cattle were domesticated millions of years before the more likely date of 7,000 to 8,000 years ago. The Charolais breed dates from the 18th century. More information: www.institut-charolais.com

→ 24 April 2002

In our piece about Ida Lupino, page 14 (Arts), April 22, we said: 'The Lupino lineage has been traced back to the Restoration, when the "Luppinos" [sic] performed as jugglers and dancers for Charles I.' That would be Charles II (Charles I did not quite make it to the Restoration).

→ 25 April 2002

In the picture on page 7, yesterday, Picasso was shown on the beach at Juan-les-Pins, not St Juan Les Pin.

→ 1 May 2002

Homophone corner: 'The mark of authenticity comes from the play-write' (Friday radio: pick of the day, G2, page 24, April 26); 'A heard of pigs' (Five years of Labour, page 9 graphic, April 27, early editions).

→ 6 May 2002

Spelling lessons: the white-plumed heron is the egret, not eagret (Ah, the pomp and pageantry, the posses and the posh suits, page 2, May 1); 'a glossy paean (not paeon, one hopes) to sex' (Springs eternal, G2, page

10, April 30). A paean is a song of praise while a paeon is 'a metrical foot of one long syllable and three short syllables' (Concise Oxford Dictionary).

→ **7 May 2002**

A headline, Dog days for the dollar (Finance, page 23, May 3), used the phrase to mean bad, or troubled times. Dog days are neutral. Collins English Dictionary defines them as follows: '1. The hot period of summer reckoned in ancient times from the heliacal rising of Sirius (the Dog Star). 2. A period marked by inactivity.'

Name changes: the late Viscount Dilhorne was Reginald Manningham-Buller, not Richard (MI5 could appoint second woman leader, page 9, April 30); Abu Ben Adhem, not Adam (Top of the class, G2, page 22, May 1); St Antony's College, Oxford, not St Anthony's (Sharon is taking us back to 1948, page 17, April 30); Walton prison, not Welton (An actor's life, G2, page 17, May 1); Paul Dirac, not Dira (Obituary: Oreste Piccioni, page 20, May 3).

→ **9 May 2002**

In our editorial about the threat to the oak tree, page 15, May 6, we misquoted David Garrick's words to the famous song. They are not 'Hearts of oak . . .' etc, but 'Heart of oak are our ships, heart of oak are our men . . .' – a reader pointed out the correct (singular) version in a letter, page 15, May 7.

In a piece headed Next challenge in space: hitching a ride on a sunbeam, page 20, May 6, we said: 'Under the pressure of the sun's rays, the spacecraft would begin accelerating at only millimetres per second, every second. But in just a day, an acceleration of 1mm per second would build up to 100 metres per second.' We should have said ' . . . and acceleration of 1mm per second per second would build up to a velocity of 100 metres per second'.

→ **11 May 2002**

A few corrections from our feature, Well read? and the list of '100 top books', pages 6 and 7, G2, May 9: it is the Book of Revelation, not Revelations (the Revelation of Saint John the Divine); it is Bel-Ami by Maupassant (not Bel Amies); it is Nineteen Eighty-Four (not 1984) it is Toni Morrison, not Tony.

→ 13 May 2002

The Brontës lived in Haworth, not Howarth, page 11, G2, May 9.

→ 20 May 2002

In our front page report, Modern women choosing to have smaller families, May 17, we said, 'Government statistics predict the number of children [in England and Wales] will fall from 21m in 2000 to 11m in 2011.' That should have said from 12.1m in 2000 to 11m in 2011.

→ 22 May 2002

The building identified as the Imperial Hotel, Vienna, page 14, yesterday, is in fact the Karlskirche, one of the city's great baroque churches.

The knarled hawthorn tree, referred to on page 24, May 20, would have become just normally gnarled

→ 23 May 2002

Ophelia is not buried hugger-mugger, as we suggested in a piece about language, Back to basics, page 23, G2, yesterday – but her father, Polonius, is. It is the king in Hamlet who says of Polonius: 'We have done but greenly in hugger-mugger to inter him.'

→ 28 May 2002

The millennium bridge to which we referred on page 1, May 24, is the Gateshead bridge rather than the Newcastle upon Tyne bridge. It is known as the 'blinking eye' not the 'blinking bridge'.

→ 31 May 2002

Mythematics corner: The Elsewhere column startled its readers, page 22, yesterday, by stating there are 56 quarters to one hundredweight. There are four quarters to a hundredweight (but there are 56 pounds in half a hundredweight).

→ 5 June 2002

A contender for the most common mistake, from page 7, of G2, a piece headed Busy syndrome: 'And you only need to nip out to the shops to

experience how "busy" mitigates against patience, tolerance, consideration and, of course, old people.' The word required there is militates, not
mitigates.

→ 7 June 2002

In our television notes, page 24, G2, June 3, we said, 'The [Buckingham
Palace] concert is followed by HRH lighting the jubilee beacon.' The
beacon was not set alight by HRH. It was done by HM.

It is not the War of Jenkin's Ear, page 6, G2, June 4. It is the War of
Jenkins' Ear, or in Guardian style, Jenkins's Ear (the 'war', between
England and Spain, 1739–41, took its name from Robert Jenkins, the
master of the Rebecca, who claimed his ear had been cut off by Spanish
coastguards: see Encyclopedia.com).

→ 8 June 2002

In a report on page 11 yesterday, we again referred to the Queen as HRH.
She is HM.

→ 12 June 2002

Contender for the most common mistake, from page 4, Sport, June 8:
'One English ex-patriot in Tokyo...' In fact, a patriotic expatriate.

→ 13 June 2002

In the opening paragraph of Trouble in paradise, page 6, G2, June 11, we
referred to 'the Saint James Bible' and 'the book of Peter'. There is no
Saint James Bible. We were thinking of the Authorised or King James
version. There is no 'book of Peter' in the Bible. But there are two Letters
or Epistles of (Saint) Peter in the New Testament. The quotation in the
article was from The First Epistle.

In our TV listings, northern editions of G2, yesterday, we said of
Ian's Big Trip (Yorkshire, 8pm): 'Ian Clayton meets Yorkshire people
who have settled in Europe'.

→ 14 June 2002

The acting chairman of the Press Complaints Commission, is not George
Pinker (Press glee over Blair's retreat, page 4, June 12). It is Professor
Robert Pinker. Apologies.

→ 15 June 2002

In a brief report, Cocaine seized in Atlantic, page 15, yesterday, we said 'One crew member of the Winner was injured when the French fired warning ships at the vessel . . .' Warning shots, in fact.

→ 18 June 2002

We helped to perpetuate the myth – in a report Jam today but what about tomorrow? page 8, June 15 – that the expression 'jam tomorrow' had something to do with the Mad Hatter's tea-party. In fact, it does not come from Alice in Wonderland at all. It comes from chapter five of Through the Looking-Glass. Here is the conversation between the White Queen and Alice: 'It's very good jam,' said the Queen. 'Well, I don't want any today, at any rate.' 'You couldn't have it if you did want it,' the Queen said. 'The rule is jam tomorrow and jam yesterday but never jam today.' 'It must come sometimes to "jam today",' Alice objected. 'No it can't,' said the Queen. 'It's jam every other day; today isn't any other day, you know.' 'I don't understand you,' said Alice. 'It's dreadfully confusing.' (The Annotated Alice, Penguin)

→ 22 June 2002

English department, from a report on page 4, June 20: 'Mr Bing cast aspersions over whether he was the father . . .' Aspersion: disparaging or malicious remark slanderous accusation . . . etc (Collins). The sense – and probably the word – required was 'doubts'.

→ 24 June 2002

In an article about Abigail's Party, pages 10 and 11, G2, June 19, we quot-ed Mike Leigh, the director, saying Alison Steadman's character, Beverly, was 'completely subdued by received notions of how we should behave and what we should have'. Mike Leigh points out that her character in fact is anything but subdued. What he actually said (in a telephone inter-view) was that Beverly was 'imbued with received notions...' etc.

An unnoticed error in a letter to the editor, page 19, yesterday, allowed the writer to say of the once disparaged holdings of 'French peasants', 'Such small mixed farms are now naturally praised as the organic ordeal.' Ideal, that would be.

→ 3 July 2002

In our report, Smoke rises over opera sponsor, page 6, July 1, we quoted the following, ' . . . I would assume smoking does cause damage to vocal chords. . . .' Earlier corrections to vocal cords still fail to strike a chord.

→ 4 July 2002

In our report about the locomotive that hit a lorry, page 9, July 2, we referred to sodium chlorate as an ingredient of fertiliser. In fact, it is an ingredient of herbicide, weedkiller, rather than fertiliser.

→ 5 July 2002

In a report, Helicopters rescue polar researchers trapped in ice, page 2, July 2, we said (in early editions only), 90 people were ferried across ice floes 'as the hours of daylight grew shorter and shorter in the past week'. In fact since the events took place in the Antarctic, the hours of daylight would have been slowly growing (while shortening in the northern hemisphere).

Whatever the characteristics of Howards End, it does not have an apostrophe (Television, page 22, G2, yesterday).

Index